# BY·PROD·UCT
## AUTONOMOUS SUCCESS IN A BOLD NEW WORLD

IAN PRUKNER

ISBN: 978-1-7327194-3-9


Book cover—Embracing Empowerment LLC

Back cover photography: Leone Combs

Cover design: Mishya Holly

Manuscript editing & Interior format—UNITED HOUSE Publishing

Interior design: Matt Russell


Produced in the United States of America

2019—First Edition


SPECIAL SALES
Embracing Empowerment LLC books are available at special quantity discounts when purchased in bulk by corporations, organizations, and special-interest groups.

For information, please e-mail info@byproductbook.com.

*This book is dedicated to all those who believed in me when I didn't,
to everybody who lit my path when it was dark,
and to everyone who refuses to give up on all they might become.*

# CONTENTS

# SECTION ONE
# THE BYPRODUCT

# 1

# THE OUTCOME IS ALWAYS FIRE

## THERE WERE NO SPARKS, JUST A GASOLINE FIRE BURNING THROUGH THE DARK.

I n a dark room, a mixture of potassium permanganate and glycerin begins to smolder; add a couple of drops of water, and fire violently erupts from the container. It's that same fire you see in the eyes of every champion, that you feel in every stunning performance, that underlies every incredible play, and that marks the soul of everyone who experiences a moment of greatness in their lives. It is also the byproduct. In both the chemical reaction of potassium permanganate with glycerin and the once in a lifetime play on the court, the FIRE is the outcome.

It's the outcome, the reaction, the byproduct, that everyone sees. The byproduct is what everyone wants. They want the fire, the win, the weight loss, the great relationship. They crave the byproduct. Everyone wants the fire, but what we really need—if we want the fire consistently—is the potassium permanganate, water, and glycerin. When combined, the outcome is ALWAYS fire. We want the win on the court, but what we need is the discipline, the practice, the thinking, and the belief that when combined, creates an unstoppable force.

Everyone wants the outcome, everyone wants greatness, everyone wants significance, purpose, and meaning. But few achieve those levels and even fewer sustain them consistently over time. This book isn't just about winning. It's about winning BIG in every area of your life that matters to you. Almost everyone can make small to moderate levels of improvement for short periods of time, but very few complete the big goals they set out to achieve. Why? They change behaviors, eat differently, go to the gym, take the class, go to the seminar. They spend time, effort, and energy chasing the outcome only to end up putting the weight back on, or going back into that destructive relationship, or falling short of their goals and dreams. Why? Could it be that when it comes to significant long-lasting success, we have been focused on the wrong things? Could it be that our understanding of what creates greatness is flawed?

We all know people who seem to live in a rain cloud. At every turn, they are met with hardship, obstacles, failure, and disappointment. We also know people that everything they touch seems to turn to gold. Their success seems almost effortless. And for the most part, it is. In both instances, their realities are being created quite naturally. It is the byproduct of who they are.

Our lives right now, the home we live in, the quality of our relationships, the measure of our health, are all byproducts. Byproducts of a reaction between our thoughts, beliefs, and actions. Our current situation is literally a perfect product of the thoughts we think, the beliefs we hold, and the actions they create. You couldn't create a more accurate or precise outcome if you tried a million times. And it's happening automatically. Winners win and losers lose, and it repeats. When you have potassium permanganate glycerin and water you get fire, every time. When you have the thoughts, beliefs, and actions that you currently hold, you get YOU every time. It's a process, a system really, that creates predictable, repeatable, and most importantly, adjustable outcomes. It is the byproduct.

The best part of the byproduct is that you don't have to learn it. You already know it. It's been working for you your entire life. All you have to do is learn to recognize it and direct it.

No matter where you are in life, this book is going to help you. Are you crushing it right now? Congratulations. We are going to clearly identify why and help you learn how to apply the byproduct process to achieve at even greater levels.

Have you been struggling for a breakthrough? This is it.

The byproduct process you are going to learn will change your life in massive ways. It works for literally everyone who uses it, precisely because you and everyone else are already using it. Twenty-four hours a day, seven days a week, the byproduct process is creating the outcomes in your life. You are already using it to obtain results, but many of us have never learned to recognize it or direct it. The process you will learn to use and apply in this book is the exact process I used to lose thirty-five pounds and keep it off for close to a decade. I used it to take my income from $27,000 a year to over seven figures a year. I've used it to create an unbelievable marriage out of a relationship filled with fighting and anger. This book is, ironically, a byproduct. It is the byproduct of the knowledge I gained and applied over a decade of leadership, people building, and delivering results in the real world. I'm not an author. I'm not some hack trying to sell you the key to success in three easy steps. I'm not some wanna-be who never did it. This IS how I did it. This is the **BYPRODUCT**.

## OUR LIVES ON AUTOPILOT

There is no political figure, no boss, and no celebrity that is going to come to your house and make your dreams come true. That is on you, so you better get after it. Today. The reason most people, most of the time, are living lives far below their potential is that they don't really understand the amount of control they actually have in directing their future. It isn't up to chance, it's up to choice and to change. Many people seem to be willing to change everything for a job. They will move, relocate the family, engage in major commutes, even change their name on social media (so their employer won't see their personal lives), yet they won't change a dad-gum thing personally to win big. For things to get better, we must get better. We must be at least as committed to our dreams as we are to our jobs. The

> **FOR THINGS TO GET BETTER, WE MUST GET BETTER.**

commitment required is the commitment to change. This book is about using the byproduct as a change agent in your life.

Currently, almost all of what you are experiencing from your financial condition to your health and the quality of your relationships is the outcome of—the perfect byproduct of—your thoughts, beliefs, and actions. You have been and always will be creating your reality. In this book, I'm going to share with you a simple but life-changing truth and the process by which it is implemented. This process is something all great achievers use and have used to create spectacular results in virtually every area of life. In my studies of high achievers and in the process of raising myself from the ranks of the average to amongst the most successful in my industry, I was able to see and describe a process which is always at work—autonomously directing our lives every moment of every day. Yet, almost everyone is unaware this process even exists, let alone how it works and how to direct it. It is, in my opinion, the single greatest connection point and the only commonality across all the fields of achievement and all great achievers. It is a most natural of occurrences. Like

> **YOU ARE NOT GOOD ENOUGH TO ACCOMPLISH YOUR DREAMS, YET.**

fire, no one has to teach it to burn. It just happens and is happening now, right now, as you read this, and will happen every moment of every day for the rest of your life. It is a never-ending force. It's like the small stream that over time carves out the great canyons from solid stone. It is relentless. This is why it is so powerful.

You are not good enough to accomplish your dreams, yet. I know this flies in the face of modern motivational leadership. Also, of course, it is in direct opposition to Chris Farley's, "I'm smart enough, I'm good enough and doggone it, people like me" speech in the movie Tommy Boy, but it's totally true. Right now, our reality is nothing more than a result which is perfectly formulated by our action or inaction. Our actions are a byproduct of our beliefs, and our beliefs are a byproduct of the thoughts we give space to in our minds. If we want to become who we might have been, we are going to have to recognize this process and harness it to create growth change in our lives.

This isn't crap put into a book to try to make someone feel better about themselves, written by, let's be honest, people who haven't done anything in life but write a book. This book is the BYPRODUCT. I didn't set out to write a book; I set out to

WIN. I embarked on a journey that has created more success than I ever imagined. I've learned a process that has helped me to produce consistent, predictable growth in virtually every area of life. It's what this book is about—creating a byproduct lifestyle where winning, whether at home, in business, on the field, or with kids is a repeatable, predictable outcome. And, get this: EVENTUALLY effortless.

How much effort does it take to be you? To react as you react? To talk how you talk? To daydream? To get in your car? None. It's natural, routine, and largely effortless. Have you ever gotten in your car only to arrive at the destination without a clue how you got there? What happened? The byproduct happened. You were able to drive a several-thousand-pound automobile 60 miles an hour with thousands of other people driving around you. You experienced constantly changing road conditions, too many variables and unknowns to possibly list, and yet you made it to your destination with minimal effort. You were making countless decisions, life and death decisions, reacting to millions of stimuli points, all with little to no effort arriving safely.

What if you could create this same level of ease and autonomy when it comes to achieving your goals and desires in other areas of your life? The answer is you can, and you do. You programmed yourself to drive your car on that route, and you can program yourself to take any other avenue in life you want. The process you are going to learn will help you identify who you are, what you want, and how to get there. Every time. And, eventually, autonomously.

## CAPTIVATING

We as a species seem to be captivated, almost drawn to true greatness. It's almost as if internally, at the deepest levels, we identify with it. It's inside all of us, and the mechanism by which it's achieved comes inborn. This is why it calls to us. It's almost as if our subconscious sees greatness and knows. It almost identifies with it in a way, and it beckons us. You don't get better by chance. You get better by CHANGE. Right now, if your thoughts were good enough, habits consistent enough, and drive strong enough to make your dreams a reality, then they would be. To get to the next level in any area of our lives we have to become more than we are now. Massive success doesn't require you to be somebody you're not. It requires you to be the best, most developed, and hungry version of you that has ever existed. Right now, no matter what level of success you have achieved, you can choose to take your game to the next level. Massive success isn't for the elite. It isn't for the few; it's for anyone, and I mean anyone, committed to change, growth, and grind at the components of this process until they become natural and autonomous. It's going to be MASSIVE WORK AT FIRST. Just like when you began driving a car, you had to be ultra-aware and ultra-sensitive at every moment. You actually came to a complete stop at the stop sign. You had to think about every action you

**YOU DON'T GET BETTER BY CHANCE.
YOU GET BETTER BY CHANGE.**

were taking. But, over time those actions became automatic. This process is the same. In the beginning, it takes effort, time, and energy to understand it, direct it, and utilize it. Once it's going in the direction you created, eventually, your results—like driving a car—become automatic.

Today, in a world demanding immediate results and microwaved success, leaders in all fields face increasing pressure to bypass the byproduct model and create results now. But, there is a difference between getting to the top and staying at the top. You might be able to shortcut your way there for a while, but ultimately, the byproduct will catch you. Talent may take you to the top, but predictable processes keep you there. Winning isn't everything, being a winner is. Coach John Wooden, former head coach at UCLA who won ten NCAA national championships, said, "When we have played the very best that we are capable of playing no scoreboard can label you a loser." Coach Wooden is also one of the greatest examples of byproduct. It took him almost ten years of perfecting his processes before he won a single championship. Once his coaching and training were dialed-in, winning was the byproduct. He later became the winningest coach in all of college sports history.

It doesn't matter where you came from, what you have or haven't done, your level of schooling, or the family you were born into. Those who are willing to learn this process of the byproduct and then overdo it, take massive action, and bring their "A" game day in and day out will rise to the top like never before in history. This book is about change, growth, and becoming the best version of yourself. It's about digging deep and creating lasting success in every area of your life. This isn't some fad, and it sure as heck isn't some theory that has never been tested. Once you see it, you will recognize its place in everything you have ever done. You will wonder why you have never seen this before.

The *BYPRODUCT* is how I took myself as a broke twenty-three-year-old earning twenty-seven thousand dollars a year to earning in excess of a million dollars a year less than a decade later—in an actual business, where real people actually had to do real work, not just taking pictures next to rented exotic cars and selling their course online on how to become insta-famous. I had to change. So will you. I had to hunt down my weaknesses, the errors in my thinking, and systematically eradicate them. I had to take long looks in the mirror, see what was broken, face everything I was not and create what I would be. You will do the same. Are you ready to win? To dig deep? To find that next gear, slam it down, and let it rip? You were made for more. There is a destiny bigger than you can imagine waiting for you on the other side of the *BYPRODUCT*.

# 2

# HOW IT WORKS

## THE AUTOMATION OF WINNING

I n this section of the book, we will look at the byproduct process and exactly how it works, why it works, and how to use it. We will also take time to understand the prerequisites required to operate it successfully. We need to not only know and understand how it works but how people work with it, use it, and relate to the process.

I'm not going to make you read all the way to the end to give you the golden nugget. It's right here, and it's almost so simple you might miss it. The rest of this book will be dedicated to teaching you everything I know and have learned about taking this process and transforming any and every area of your life for the better. It seems simple on the surface, but underneath, there is an ocean of richness, texture, and color which will help you gain understanding, control, and mastery of this incredible tool.

# THE BYPRODUCT PROCESS

Our lives are created by the following process:

Thoughts become beliefs,

Beliefs become actions (or inactions),

Actions become results.

This process has created virtually every reality in our lives. It's happening all of the time, operating below our radar and bringing us what we think about, what we most desire, and what we act upon. From this point forward, we will refer to the BYPRODUCT PROCESS (thoughts become beliefs, beliefs become actions, and actions become results) as the TBAR process (Thought Beliefs Actions Results). We will also use TBAR and BYPRODUCT process interchangeably throughout the duration of the book.

# THE TBAR REACTION

Inputs create the outcome.

Potassium permanganate + glycerin + water (inputs) = FIRE (byproduct). The input creates the byproduct.

Take something out of the prior equation, and you don't get fire. You get something completely different and a lot less spectacular. And that's kind of how life works. We can have almost all the ingredients, we can be 90% of the way there, but no fire. We all want the flame, but, what we should seek instead, are the inputs that create the fire.

Our thoughts are always producing beliefs as their byproduct.

Our beliefs are always producing actions or inactions as their byproduct.

Our actions are always producing results as their byproduct.

Our organizations, churches, and companies all follow the same process too. Look at the behavior of an organization, does it mimic the core values of the entity? If not, those values aren't really values; they are just nice thoughts which have not made their way into the beliefs, hearts, and culture of the organization. Growing an organization is just like growing ourselves. When we focus on the inputs, the outcomes take care of themselves. If we want to grow our church, company, or community group, we start by growing our people. The people grow the organization. When we work on how our people think, the belief sets, values, and culture they produce, we will move the business. Culture is the "belief" of the organization, and just like for individuals, it is working twenty-four hours a day. It creates the actions we take and the results we get.

Here are a few positive examples of this process in action:

**Thinking (T)**

I desire to change my life, specifically in the area of health and well-being. I have a goal to lose thirty pounds and keep it off. I can imagine what I will look like and feel like when the thirty pounds are gone. I have observed many others from many different backgrounds of life lose weight. I think if they could do it, I could do it as well. I am willing to put in the time and effort to lose weight. I am willing to learn the process and take the necessary actions. In observing others, I notice patterns of behavior, actions, and attitudes which seem consistent across the different examples of successful weight loss. I recognize many of my actions and choices are not in alignment with the examples of success I have been observing.

**These thoughts become beliefs (B)**

I believe, if others did this, I can learn what they did and imitate it. I believe this is learnable. I believe the tradeoff of time and effort will be worth it. I believe the reward will be greater than the cost in the way I look and feel. I believe if I did what others are doing, in the same amounts and with the same consistency, I would have similar results because I believe in cause and effect. I also believe my choices got me where I am and won't get me where I want to be. If I were doing the right things, I would already have the right results.

**These beliefs lead to action (A)**

I begin to study the examples of success in this area thoroughly, looking for cause and effect relationships. I examine my actions against the standards of success and make necessary course corrections. I change my diet, and I exercise regularly. I build relationships with others who have similar goals to help keep me accountable. I track my progress against my goal and seek out coaching when my results don't line up with my expectations.

**These actions lead to results (R)**

Because I ate fewer calories and burned more calories, more consistently, I lost weight. Given enough time or an increase in calorie burn, my thirty-pound weight loss becomes an inevitability. Not an "if" but a "when."

Your results create a REINFORCEMENT of your initial thoughts and beliefs. The thoughts you developed and the changes you applied are confirmed in your results. Your thinking and belief systems—having been validated by your experience—become deeply held truths. They more easily create the action in the future which created the result you wanted. You have started the cycle of success. See the graphic below for a visual representation of the success cycle.

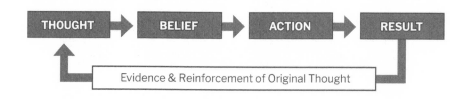

Let's take a look at the exact same situation but with a different set of TBAR inputs.

### Thinking (T)

I desire to change my life, specifically in the area of weight loss. I desire to lose 30 pounds. I think losing weight is hard. I say: "I've tried before, and it's never worked. I don't like the food I have to eat, and you only live once, right?" I need to enjoy myself once in a while. I know other people have lost weight, but I am different because of X, Y, and Z. I have a harder time working out, so it doesn't work as well for me. I am just big boned. I'm really busy at work and with the kids, so I'm not sure how I will fit this in. Others who succeed must not have the life responsibilities I have. It must be nice.

### These thoughts become beliefs (B)

There is more to losing weight than it appears. What works for others probably won't work for me. I can put in the work, but it still may not work for me because I'm big boned. I just don't have the genetics to be really fit. If I were at a different place in my life, it would be easier. I will try, but I don't really expect it to work.

### These beliefs lead to action (A)

I go to the gym a few times. I eat a salad for lunch a couple of times, but I'm not totally committed, so my results are slow. I am sore afterward and wonder if I am doing it wrong; I must be doing it wrong. Since I don't believe it

> **IN YOUR MIND, YOU HAVE TRIED, AND IT DIDN'T WORK. IT DOESN'T OCCUR TO YOU THAT YOU DIDN'T WORK.**

will really work for me, I never bother to study the people who are where I want to be. Instead of looking to them for wisdom, I simply dismiss their success to luck, genes, or a lifestyle I don't think is attainable for me. Instead of getting feedback from those ahead of me, I become my own feedback loop. I get discouraged and eventually go back to the life I had before trying to make the change.

### These actions create results (R)

I didn't lose much weight at all. I was just really sore and had to eat salad for lunch, which I hate anyway. I don't see my lack of success as being related to unrealistic expectations about what it was going to take to achieve the goal. The lack of results couldn't have been from an inconsistent, fatalistic approach to the change. Rather, I see it as a reinforcement of my current thinking and belief that losing weight is hard and I am not like others. In your mind, you have tried, and it didn't work. It doesn't occur to you that YOU didn't work. It is the reinforcement of your current thoughts, beliefs, and actions which cement them even deeper into your subconscious. This makes the existing result more and more concrete in your life. Your entire life will change when you get ahold of the TBAR process and the mechanism by which you direct it. Any vision you have for your life can be broken down, internalized, and acted upon to bring it to reality.

# PROCESS BREAKDOWN

## DISRUPTING THE PROCESS

N ow that we know how the TBAR process works, we will discuss some of the common pitfalls associated with it. There is a DANGER within the TBAR process. The power and pitfall of the TBAR process is, it works too well. It produces such accurate and consistent results that we are in danger of using it as a negative self-fulfilling prophecy. In the example from the previous chapter, the negative result is exactly what is created from negative thinking. The result is so well-tied to the thinking and belief which created it. And, if we don't evaluate our outcomes, thinking, and our understanding of cause and effect—then identify the fallacies in our thinking and belief systems—we will create consistently negative outcomes in our lives. We must examine ourselves, our thinking, and our desires. We must hold them to a standard to create alignment between them.

It's important to understand you can, and people often do, attempt to interrupt and redirect a part of the process. They interrupt the process by trying to add an input closer to the actual byproduct they are trying to change. Instead of starting at the beginning of the reaction, working on creating new and better thinking, people often try to work on creating change at the action level.

The most common example of this is when people attempt to abruptly change their actions without changing the beliefs used to create them. They begin suddenly going to the gym more, making extra sales calls, or unexpectedly trying to stop smoking or drinking—all in an attempt to change the result. And for some time, if the action is changed significantly enough, the result changes. However, if the underlying thoughts and beliefs are not consciously directed and reprogrammed into more accurate inputs, eventually a relapse will occur. Typically, stress or something disrupting the pace or state of life will cause us to revert to our existing operating system. A death, a new career, a new relationship, or a financial windfall—all of these interrupt our conscious redirection of action, and we fall back to our underlying programming. While interruption can help accelerate change, the change will only be lasting when partnered with the purposeful programming of the inputs of TBAR process.

People who try to change the result at the action level are almost certainly bound to experience limited success. For example, think about someone who is trying to lose weight and live a healthier lifestyle. They begin this journey by deciding to change their actions instead of changing the thinking which caused the weight gain. They begin eating right and going to the gym but do not address the underlying thoughts and beliefs that caused the years of inaction and indifference. They lose weight for a while, they live healthy for a while, but then something comes up, and they revert to the same unhealthy person they were before, often putting all the weight (and possibly more) back on. Why is this? Because TRUE LASTING CHANGE does not occur at the action or behavior level. It occurs at the thinking and belief level. It becomes a new subconscious mode of operating, and the new belief creates new behavior. While most of us disdain going to the gym, ask any great athlete, and you will find it's just what they do. In contrast, an old belief with a new, unnatural behavior never creates that sort of automation, and doing the new activities always feels like work.

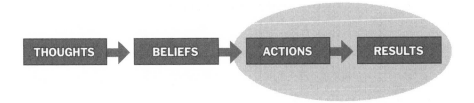

According to this diagram, what is most directly responsible for the result?

The action.

Most people have an idea of what they want (a thought). They can picture their ideal weight, their ideal income, their ideal relationship, but have no mechanism to make it a reality. Having the desired outcome, and looking for a way to obtain it, most people can correctly identify their action as the most direct cause of their results. This creates attempts to make a correction at the action level. They join a gym (take action). They enroll in a class (take action), or they see a marriage counselor (take action). The action is helpful for a while, but almost always, we abandon our new actions for action that looks eerily similar to our original actions.

Why? We fail to realize the result we are getting currently is the byproduct of a very natural action for us. And the action is the byproduct of our underlying beliefs. Unless the beliefs change, they will continue to produce automatically, the byproduct action we have been acting with already. The belief is where the action came from. Changing the belief is really the only way to change the action long range. A change in belief can only be accomplished by a change in the range and pattern of our thoughts. Think about it like this:

The thought is the input. The byproduct of the thought is the belief. The belief then becomes the input to the next step in the process and creates the byproduct of action. The action then acts as the input which creates the byproduct of the result.

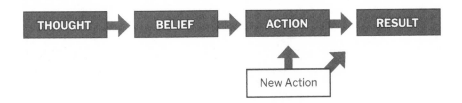

When we willfully choose a different input in the middle of the equation, it is an unnatural occurrence. It wasn't created by the step before. It is totally new. Like how a body often rejects an organ transplant, the success process rejects any input over time when it is unnaturally injected.

We will always compete with naturally occurring behavior when we try to exert change at the behavior or action level. This behavior is being created by the existing thoughts and beliefs which create conflict! This is called cognitive dissonance and is where most lose the battle in lasting change.

Injected change—change which is inserted in the middle of the TBAR process—happens on a conscious level. Conscious choice requires focus, attention, and effort. It is not naturally occurring and therefore requires effort to maintain. Distractions and stress can cause a loss of focus. When we stop focusing on the

> **WE WILL ALWAYS COMPETE WITH NATURALLY OCCURRING BEHAVIOR WHEN WE TRY TO EXERT CHANGE AT THE BEHAVIOR OR ACTION LEVEL.**

conscious change, the underlying operating system takes over again. When the change isn't being consciously monitored, the underlying autopilot (the outcome of the thoughts and beliefs) take over. these exist at a subconscious level. These existing thoughts and beliefs are our operating system so to speak. They represent our default setting. They are consistent and effortless. The subconscious is an extremely powerful yet largely unharnessed tool.

Think again about your drive home. You pull out into traffic listening to your favorite podcast when another driver tries moving into your lane. Almost instantly you slam on the breaks. You swerve into another lane and become acutely aware. In this split second, you don't say to yourself, "Tricep adjust thirty degrees and contract, the right calf squeeze, the right foot moves down with 30 pounds of pressure and apply for two seconds to the break..."

You are not giving yourself conscious direction. Your subconscious, in an effort to keep you alive, is operating in alignment with your thoughts and beliefs that being alive is good. It controls your body enabling you to make split-second, gut-level reactions to save your life. Much in the same way, your subconscious is making split-second gut-level judgments and reactions every minute of every day. It happens naturally, it's the byproduct of your thoughts and beliefs. If you don't change the original source of the input, your subconscious will continue to act on the belief it has and will continue to give you exactly what you've got now, over and over again, every time. If you want lasting change, it must become the byproduct of a different way of thinking.

The secret to most achievement is actually no secret at all. It's the ability to observe the natural occurrences around us, understand what caused them, and then harness and direct them in our lives. When we get results-focused instead of input-focused, we lose. When we get input-focused, we win. It's that simple. Think about the old adage where no one wants a drill, what they really want is a hole. The drill is merely the mechanism by which the hole is created. The drill – the input. The hole is the byproduct of the drill. Buy the drill, and you can have as many holes as you like. Want a hole but don't buy the drill, and you will have a hard time creating what you desire.

We want to lose weight, so we diet. Diets are great but what about addressing the thoughts and beliefs that allowed us to get overweight to begin with? We want a better relationship, so we read a book on how to improve it. This is a step in the right direction, but are we exploring the thinking and beliefs we hold which have allowed our relationship to deteriorate?

THOUGHT ➤ BELIEF ➤ ACTION ➤ RESULT

Imagine the TBAR process represented by diagonal lines. The "lined" thought created a "lined" belief, the "lined" belief created a "lined" action, and the "lined" action created a "lined" result.

To create lasting change, we must start by changing the first step in the reaction. If all you change are the later steps, you still have the original "lined" result being created, and the final byproduct becomes a strange blend.

Imagine the "lined" TBAR process creating the "lined" result. We decide to add a "dotted" action over the "lined" action, hoping to yield us a "dotted" result. As you see below at the action level, we now have two actions, the new "dotted" action and the existing "lined" action. Why? Because the inputs creating it are still present. All we have done is interject an action on top of it (the "dotted" action on the "lined"). Instead of getting the "dotted" result we desire, we get a mix of the "dotted" and "lined" result. Why? The earlier inputs were not replaced and thus continued to produce their natural byproducts.

You get some really odd results as outcomes when you mix inputs along the way. This is predominately why rational, capable people can end up with disastrous lives. They don't account for the mixing of the inputs. Remember, the byproduct is ALWAYS being produced from the input before it.

THOUGHTS ➤ BELIEFS ➤ ACTIONS ➤ RESULTS

New Action

## THE FALLACY OF FEELINGS

Feelings aren't a part of the process. Our modern society is overly dependent and fixated on feelings. If you feel like doing it, do it. If you don't, don't. If you feel offended, you have a right to attack what offends you, even if it violates the rights of others. Here's the truth—FEELINGS ARE LIARS. They can change as easily as the wind, so don't follow them unless you don't care where you end up. Get out of your feelings, there ain't no money in there.

A feeling is something which usually happens in response to an external situation. It's a reaction, and generally isn't a byproduct of the TBAR process. The issue with unchecked feelings is they mix with the process and create unexpected outcomes similar to the process interruptions discussed earlier.

Feelings are emotional responses to interpretations of outside circumstances. They bypass the TBAR process and interject themselves in the place of beliefs. People act on feelings all the time in ways they later regret. When someone acts on a feeling, they almost never come out with the result they wanted. Think about the person who feels a physical and emotional attraction to someone who doesn't carry similar thought and belief systems. We have all known people who get married to someone seemingly incompatible. They marry someone they are attracted to but who has fundamentally different thought processes, only to watch the marriage end in irreconcilable differences down the road. The attraction may be

**GET OUT OF YOUR FEELINGS, THERE AIN'T NO MONEY IN THERE.**

very real, but over time, the byproduct of the belief systems overrides the initial attraction. Years go by, and the attraction fades. All that's left are the naturally occurring byproducts and the thought, "I didn't know I was marrying someone like this."

Since the interjection of feelings is not part of the byproduct process, they are not accountable to that process. What does this mean? As so many of us will attest, there isn't a steady, predictable, repeatable pattern creating the feeling. When we take action or inaction based on our feelings, we will create unpredictable and non-repeatable outcomes. Frequently, our emotional reactions to circumstances are in direct opposition to our thoughts and beliefs. We want one thing, but we act out on emotion in a way contrary to what we want. We want to be successful at work, but an emotional outburst during a heated staff meeting limits our success. Acting on emotions can create dangerous outcomes. For example, a young entrepreneur understands that his vision will be met along the way with many setbacks. However, he holds the belief that the challenges along the way allow him to learn, get better, grow, and actually help him to succeed. When, on the journey, the young entrepreneur finds himself in the middle of a highly emotional letdown, he may still be tempted to give up. But, giving up would be an act in opposition to the belief that he will accomplish the dream eventually. At that moment, the feeling of pain and defeat urges him to quit, throw in the towel, or re-evaluate his commitment. None of these are byproducts of the entrepreneur's underlying thinking and belief systems. They are simply emotional reactions to outside circumstances. Feelings cause us to make permanent decisions based on temporary situations. You must be vigilant

> **FEELINGS CAUSE US TO MAKE PERMANENT DECISIONS BASED ON TEMPORARY SITUATIONS.**

to guard against the tyranny of feelings. There's going to be many opportunities every single day to be derailed by them. There's going to be plenty of things you don't feel like doing, but you've got to do them anyways. My advice: Suck it up, Buttercup, nobody cares about your feelings, only your results.

## THE CATALYST OF CRITICISM

Quit waiting for people to support you. Most of them can't even support themselves. Another danger to the TBAR process is the interjected emotions resulting from criticism. If you ever do anything worthwhile in life, you will attract critics. If you aren't being criticized now, get ready it's coming. The only way to avoid criticism is to do nothing, have nothing, and be nothing. The higher you climb on the ladder of success, the more visible you become and the more criticism you will attract.

> **WHEN YOU BUY OTHER PEOPLES' OPINIONS, YOU ALSO BUY THEIR LIFESTYLE, SO BUYER BEWARE.**

It's important to not let the negative emotions associated with unjust and unfair criticism disrupt your TBAR process. Consider if you were to become the President of the United States, the most powerful person in the world. On your very first day on the job, before you have had any chance to prove yourself or enact one policy, over fifty percent of Americans will hate you. Criticism is par for the course of a leader. But remember this— not all criticism is created equal.

**Consider the Source**

When you buy other peoples' opinions, you also buy their lifestyle, so buyer beware.

Ultimately, when we accept criticism or let it get to us, we are interrupting our TBAR process and interjecting the critic's thought or belief in place of our own. This thought or belief will eventually affect our actions and results. If we don't desire the results the critic has achieved, we need to dismiss the criticism. Remember this—generally, the loudest criticisms come from the cheapest seats.

> **CONSTRUCTIVE CRITICISM IS A POWERFUL TOOL IN THE ARSENAL OF ANY REAL LEADER.**

One of the hardest critics to dismiss can be well-meaning friends and family. If you stand in a garage it doesn't make you a car. Similarly, just because someone is close to you relationally, does not make them an expert worthy of criticizing you. Generally, the people who are closest to you want the best for you, but they probably aren't qualified to give the advice or criticism they are offering. In my experience, the people most often responsible for killing the dreams and desires of others are those closest to them. Unaware of exactly what they are doing, they project their own limited understanding and beliefs on others.

## Evaluate the Fruit

If someone has expertise and experience in the area they are critiquing, it is worth taking the time to understand what they are saying and why they are saying it. Constructive criticism is a powerful tool in the arsenal of any real leader. As we will discuss in future chapters, constructive criticism and feedback are invaluable course-correctors along our path, helping to guide us through our blind spots and other potential areas of misdirection.

One of the personal approaches I have taken to criticism from trusted sources is, every criticism contains a seed of truth within it. One of the keys to success is to be willing to dig that seed of truth out and plant it in our lives. The byproduct will be a harvest of success. Criticism from mentors and other leaders

> **EVERY CRITICISM CONTAINS A SEED OF TRUTH WITHIN IT.**

shouldn't just be listened to but should be actively sought out and applied. Criticism from mentors and people with proven track records of success can boost our self-awareness and help us to rapidly eliminate or improve upon the blind spots that hinder us. Learn from the constructive critics, but ultimately, it's okay to be disliked or misunderstood; not everyone is going to agree with you. Stand for what you believe in. If you know what you are doing is correct, then who cares what others think. Every bit of human progress has been opposed at some point by small minds.

## ISOLATING THE ISSUE

Whenever we experience a loss, failure, or frustration in accomplishing our desired outcome, there is always a reason. The setback or obstacle is being caused by something. Your ability to accurately identify the cause and act on replacing and reprogramming it will be a major catalyst to your success.

As we raise our awareness of both the TBAR process and ourselves, we can more easily understand the reasons for our successes and failures and how to isolate the underlying cause and effect which is creating our outcomes. This is an incredibly powerful tool to have ownership of. If you ask people who aren't winning in life the reason why they lack success, they can sincerely answer that they don't know. If you don't know what's wrong, how can you fix it? Using the TBAR process to isolate and identify problem areas makes the solution to those obstacles clear.

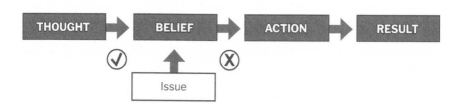

One of the greatest benefits of understanding the TBAR process is that it reveals the truth and gives us data about areas for improvement. For example, think of someone you know who talks a big game but whose actions don't match their words. Looking at the TBAR process, the thinking looks good, but the corresponding action isn't happening. If the thought never makes its way to the action, the problem lies in the belief part of the equation. Understanding this process will allow you to isolate the areas acting as blockers to your desired outcome. In the above example, the conscious desire for change has not made its way into the subconscious as a belief. The new thought has not happened strongly enough or often enough to replace and reprogram the existing belief. Which is why it never creates the corresponding action.

## REPLACE AND REPROGRAM

Once you have successfully isolated a problem area in the TBAR process, you can begin replacing and reprogramming. As we have previously discussed, interjecting new actions at the action level of the sequence is not in and of itself a long-range solution. Most of the replacement and reprogramming will happen at the level of thought and belief. Since beliefs are the byproduct of thought, we will center our discussion here around the replacement and reprogramming of our current thoughts.

When replacement and reprogramming happen on this level, it eventually works its way through the entire TBAR process. This creates new and different outcomes by design. The replacement and reprogramming process allows us to move from passive outcomes, i.e., what we have, to active outcomes (i.e. what we choose). We create

> WE GO FROM LIVING LIFE BY DEFAULT TO LIVING LIFE BY DESIGN WHEN WE CHOOSE OUR INPUTS INSTEAD OF PASSIVELY ACCEPTING THEM.

the byproducts we want by selecting and downloading the inputs which create them. We go from living life by default to living life by design when we choose our inputs instead of passively accepting them.

### The Reprogramming Process

The first step in the process of reprogramming is to identify the thoughts which are creating unwanted beliefs, actions, and outcomes.

33

Most people are aware of their own negative tendencies and the thoughts behind them. In case you believe you don't have them, ask your spouse, a mentor, or a co-worker if they can help you identify some of the thinking that may be responsible for negative outcomes in your life.

Earlier in my life, I suffered from mild hypochondria. Hypochondria is a condition where you constantly think you are sick. Multiple times I ended up in the emergency room with the symptoms I had just viewed on the latest episode of *E.R.* or *Dr. Quinn, Medicine Woman.* (I know, I know. But Dr. Quinn was a boss.) After spending another night and into the early hours of the morning in the emergency room with all the symptoms of what I had just seen but with perfectly clear test results,

> **IF GROWTH AND HEALTH AND WHOLENESS ARE OUR NATURAL STATE, THEN SICKNESS, WORRY, AND DECLINE ARE NOT.**

I had had enough. I began to take my thoughts captive and to replace and reprogram. I started keeping track of my thinking. 300-400 times a day I would have thoughts about being sick: *That didn't feel right, what was that? This doesn't seem right! I probably have this…* The first step was to identify the thoughts creating the byproduct issue.

The second step was to replace them with different thinking. Every time I had one of those negative thoughts, I immediately replaced it, most of the time in my mind, but out loud if it were possible. I would say, "That's not my thought." First Peter 2:24b (NIV) says that "by your [Jesus] wounds I am healed. I have been given life and health to all of my body. I am healthy, whole, and healed." For me, I leaned on the truth of the Bible for the replacement thought. If growth and health and wholeness are our natural state, then sickness, worry, and decline are not. A false thought making its way through the byproduct process will manifest very real but wrong outcomes in our lives. When we replace the false thought with one of truth, the byproduct process begins to change.

Once we have identified the problem thinking and created a suitable replacement, we must reprogram. 300/400 times a day, the wrong thought was being programmed into my mind, through constant repetition, or what best-selling, self-help author

Napoleon Hill calls auto-suggestion. The thought of sickness had been programmed into my subconscious belief to the point where I was expecting to see, and searching for, symptoms in line with the negative thoughts I held. Literally, every time I had one of those thoughts surface, I would speak the new thought in its place. 300-400 times a day I would repeat my new thoughts. For the first several days, nothing really changed, however within about three weeks, all of the symptoms and worry had subsided. Within about six weeks, virtually all the negative thoughts were gone, and in their place were the new truths I had reprogrammed. When I felt negative symptoms, my gut reaction was now one of healing and wholeness instead of a visualization of the worst-case scenario. For over fifteen years I have been totally symptom and issue free. This process of reprogramming works with literally any thought you want to change.

In summary, replacement and reprogramming happen in the following process:

1. Identify the problem thought.

2. Create a replacement thought.

3. Repeat this thought as often and intensely as possible until it is accepted by our subconscious.

The same process is useable at the belief and action level. Identify a belief or action that needs to change. Identify a replacement belief or action, and then repeat it as often as necessary to lodge it into your subconscious operating system. Remember, our beliefs are not filtering truth, they are simply accepting what is repeated often and vividly enough.

Write down three thoughts you need to replace—are you thinking about what you are thinking about?

1. _____

2. _____

3. _____

Write out the three replacement thoughts.

1. _____

2. _____

3. _____

Write out three beliefs which need to be replaced—are your beliefs serving you?

1. _____

2. _____

3. _____

Write out the three replacement beliefs you want to hold instead.

1. _____

2. _____

3. _____

Write out three actions which need to change for you to accomplish your goal.

1. _____

2. _____

3. _____

Write out the three actions which will replace your current actions.

1. _____

2. _____

3. _____

Keep track every day how many times your mind is pulled back into its current thought, belief, and action patterns. Every time this happens, replace and reprogram. Sooner than you think, the outcomes in your life will begin to change.

# SECTION TWO
# HOW WE WORK

# 4

# CAUSE AND EFFECT

## CONNECT THE DOTS

**W**e live in a world of cause and effect, governed by natural law with repeatable outcomes. Yet, most people can't seem to connect the dots in their life. There are people who honestly desire change but are clueless about what is actually affecting their reality. They look outside themselves to circumstances, politicians, family members, or bad breaks as the reason for their lack of results. The truth is, while outside circumstances play a role, how we interpret them (our thoughts about what we experience) is completely within our control. There

> **THERE ARE PEOPLE WHO HAVE GONE THROUGH WHAT YOU HAVE GONE THROUGH AND STILL WIN.**

are people who have gone through what you have gone through and still win. There are people who started with far less than any of us and are crushing life. Why? The THOUGHTS they think, their responses, and world view create favorable byproducts.

Consider a forest; every tree grew from a seed. The seed took the natural resources around it and grew into a towering oak, all without a life coach, a motivational speaker, or a seven-step program. Why? Because that's what it's programmed to do, GROW. Everywhere around you, there is naturally occurring growth. It's how humans are naturally programmed, too. As newborns, we don't make conscious choices. Our subconscious operating system is in control; it tells us what we need and when we need it. We don't beat around the bush and obsess about what others might think of us if we make our request known. Our natural programming demands it. It tells us we need sleep, so we sleep. We are born with it.

For most of us, somewhere along the way, the natural programming gets interrupted by thoughts and beliefs put into us by well-meaning but unqualified individuals. It may be a parent, a teacher, or a friend who gives us the destructive thinking patterns which ultimately destroy our dreams. Remember this—God didn't make losers. We learned how to lose all on our own. Losing outcomes are the result of losing thinking. You can't

> **GOD DIDN'T MAKE LOSERS. WE LEARNED HOW TO LOSE ALL ON OUR OWN.**

win in life while losing in your mind. In sports psychologist Tim Grover's book *Relentless*, he says that we are "born relentless, but taught to relent". Along the way, we abandon the natural relentlessness and thinking which creates growth and success in our lives. In its place, incorrect thinking and world views which stop the growth and hinder success creep in. Growth is natural and occurs as a byproduct of RIGHT AND TRUE THINKING. Stagnation is the natural byproduct of incorrect thinking or falsehood accepted in the belief system.

For example, a successful businessman thinks the traits of successful people can be understood, learned from, and applied in creating his own success. His thoughts create the belief that he can achieve whatever he is willing to learn and implement. His thought creates a belief which causes him to take action and create his desired result. This reinforces his original thought that things can be observed, learned, applied and achieved.

In contrast, an unsuccessful person would like to be successful but thinks success is largely to do with luck. Since he believes himself unlucky, there is no point in observing, learning, and applying the successful traits of others. He thinks, What will that matter anyway? The lack of observing, learning, and applying leaves him unable to create the success he wants. His outcome is a reinforcement of the thought that success is really about luck. This is the problem with unexamined thinking: Without holding our results to a standard, we will ALWAYS receive feedback from the world which reinforces our original thought. This occurs because the result is always the byproduct of the thought. The thought creates the belief which creates the action which creates the outcome. ALWAYS. Not sometimes. ALWAYS. Unless we are willing to ask the question, "Are my thoughts serving me?" and hold our thoughts to the standard that right thoughts create right results, we are unable to detect the thinking holding us back!

## ACCURATE AWARENESS

We are masters at self-deception. We can't change what we aren't aware is holding us back. In his book *177 Mental Toughness Secrets of the World Class*, Steve Siebold discusses the idea of four levels of awareness. He relates them to socioeconomic classes. The socioeconomic classes are really the byproduct of the thinking and belief systems held within the classes. Let's take a look at Siebold's four levels of awareness:

1. **Poverty** – People operating at this level of awareness are generally in survival mode and living in a harsh set of circumstances. They generally aren't concerned with long-range planning or creating pathways to a better life; they are simply trying to get by. They spend most of their time reacting to their environment. At this level, there's not a lot of accurate thought occurring about why one is there, it's just accepted as what is, and life goes on. There is an underlying victimhood belief which discourages people at this level of awareness from taking control of their lives. They believe the system is rigged against them and completely discount their ability to change their circumstances.

2. **Working Class** – This level of awareness is marked by the status quo. *This is how we have always done things, and this is how we will do them in the future.* This thinking longs for the good old days when our dated skill sets

and beliefs were enough. Change and growth are not readily accepted, as people at this level wish for the way things were. Their thinking and belief systems don't adapt well to the changing environments. While they are hard workers, they usually don't see the connection between results and compensation. They typically aren't concerned with raising any higher in life, and nobody around them is, either.

3. **Middle Class** – This level of awareness operates at a high enough level to understand that higher levels exist. This is a cause of great frustration. Their primary motivations are comfort and security. They value titles, degrees, and fitting in. They are highly concerned with the thoughts and opinions of others. They tend to operate in a "what's in it for me" sort of mentality. They never spend time critically evaluating the differences in thinking, belief, and action between people at their level and people at higher levels. They attribute people at higher level success to luck, greed, the right family, and opportunities. "Victim" is the watchword for those people who use what they personally didn't have as a reason to stop themselves from developing into everything they are capable to become.

4. **World Class** – This awareness level sees things clearly and as they are. They understand people pay for value and solutions. The bigger the problem, the more valuable the solution. They spend their lives in the service of other people and solving people's most pressing problems. They learn to be incredible managers of assets and extraordinary leaders of people. Their ability to see things accurately and consistently allows them to produce the results that have catapulted them to the top of their field, whether in sports, business, or at home. These champions have identified the thinking, beliefs, and actions which lead to results.

Are we aware of the dots connecting around us? Do we accurately see the cause and effect relationship of the TBAR process creating our outcomes?

# 5

# WHO WE ARE

**M**any people suffer from an acute and severe lack of awareness of who and how they are as an individual. When our view of ourselves and others is inaccurate or incomplete, it makes it harder for us to understand why the world is working in the way it is. Our ability to relate to the world and those in it and to create the results we want is dramatically hindered.

The ability to clearly understand cause and effect helps us to understand and direct the TBAR process. The ability to understand ourselves and how we interact with the process allows us to direct it forcefully and accurately.

How many times have we struggled with some new piece of technology, swearing something must not be working? After hours on tech support, we find out the problem wasn't the technology, it was us. Our inability to interact with the technology correctly limited its use in our lives. Nothing was

> **WHEN WE CHALK SUCCESS UP TO LUCK, WE CHALK OUR LIVES UP TO MEDIOCRITY.**

wrong with it; the problem was how we were using or relating to it. The TBAR process operates much the same way. It works, but if we aren't careful to know ourselves and some of the common points of user error, it will have limited impact and usability in our lives.

When we see ourselves and others as we are, not as we wish to be, we have the ability to utilize the process clearly and accurately. Think about this example: at work, you view yourself as a no-nonsense leader who gets things done. All of your coworkers view you as overbearing and a micromanager. Your incorrect view of yourself (a belief) causes you to take incorrect action (more overbearing and micromanaging), which leads to less than anticipated team engagement and results. Without seeing ourselves as we really are, we may never find the answer to our troubled outcome because we can't see ourselves as the problem. Only when we see ourselves accurately are all our cards really on the table and incredible results become possible.

For further thought, consider this husband and his wife. He loves to give her gifts. To him, it shows he thinks about her and is a representation of his love for her. She does not really look at the gifts the same way; in fact, she could live without them. What she could really use, and would mean a lot to her, is a hand around the house. He believes he is communicating love and showing his wife the affection she needs because giving gifts is how he shows love. However, she doesn't feel loved because the way love is being communicated to her isn't aligning with her expectations. Fighting continues in the household with both of them clueless about why they are having such a difficult time. *Doesn't she see how I feel about her?* he thinks. *Why can't he just pick up a little slack around the house?* she thinks. Our inability to know ourselves and to truly know the people around us creates inaccurate assumptions and inputs. Those inputs create undesired negative results.

## KNOW THYSELF FOR HE IS THINE ENEMY

One of the greatest tools I have seen to create awareness of self and others is called the Johari window. Used frequently in the world of personal coaching, the Johari window helps us to identify and have conversations around our "four selves," the total of the four selves being our true and accurate self.

Let's take a look at the diagram below.

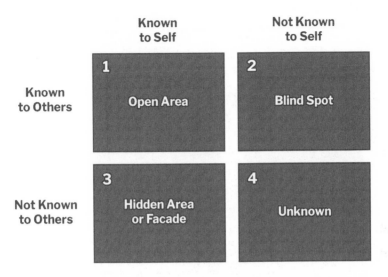

**THE JOHARI WINDOW MODEL**

Let's dive into each of the four panels of the Johari window.

1. **The Evident Self - The Open Area** – Known to self and known to others. This is the evident you, the personality traits known to you and to others. This is the you in plain sight for all to see. This is your short temper, your wit, your work ethic or lack thereof, that you and everyone else around you knows about. There is no façade; what you see is what you get. This is the area in our life where we possess an awareness of who we are, how we act, what our strengths and weaknesses are, and our tendencies, In the evident self-quadrant, others know these things as well. There are no secrets here and no fooling anyone. This is our true self. It is the byproduct of who we are.

2. **The Blind Self - Blind Spot** – things others know about us that we do not know. This quadrant of the Johari window is the most relevant to our discussion on the TBAR process. In this quadrant, our traits and characteristics are perceived by others, but not by us. This lack of awareness of self is a major contributor to the negative outcomes we experience in our lives.

The blind self is the area which can be enriched by constructive criticism. Think of a guy who constantly interrupts. No one likes talking to him, but he can't understand why. Anybody who talks to him for five minutes knows that his behavior in conversation is abrasive, but the interrupter is honestly unaware of this bad habit. Have you ever met someone with a glaring issue in some area of their life? Everyone around them can see the issue, but they themselves can't seem to recognize it. This is the blind spot, and we all have them. Sometimes, recurring themes of criticism can bring to light blind spots in our lives. Criticism in this area helps to make us aware and can be the first step in creating the clarity necessary to change and grow.

The blind self gives light to the phenomenon that we are able to unknowingly hold false thoughts and ideas about ourselves and then act on them for others to see, while personally remaining unaware of them. Back to the conversation interrupter. He believes his ideas need to be heard and that everyone else finds them valuable when really, everyone else finds his interrupting rude and annoying. Because he is blind to this piece of his personality, but others are not, his false beliefs about himself will continue to generate actions that are not in his best interest. He continues to hold the false belief and act in ways that undermine his desire to be liked and respected by the group. Whenever we are allowed to hold false beliefs about ourselves, we will always see those beliefs manifest into undesirable results. The Johari window allows the participant to begin to ask the tough question: "What do others know about me that I

> **WHENEVER WE ARE ALLOWED TO HOLD FALSE BELIEFS ABOUT OURSELVES, WE WILL ALWAYS SEE THOSE BELIEFS MANIFEST INTO UNDESIRABLE RESULTS.**

don't know?" The person who activity solicits feedback about their blind spots and shortcomings is light years ahead of the competition when it comes to creating lasting change and success with the TBAR process. Criticism, especially in the area of our blind spots, can be one of the greatest assets of the potential achiever. It helps to quickly develop awareness in an area that could be holding them back, which they may have otherwise never discovered. This quickens the TBAR process, helping us to create success more rapidly than previously possible. More about the Blind Spot shortly.

3. **The Façade Self - The Hidden Area** – The hidden self. Known to us but not to others. This is the mask we all wear. It is the side of us we would rather not bring to light. It's our deepest, most personal thoughts, desires, and secrets. It is that which we shroud in mystery from the lives and sight of others. It's the person with the drinking problem who hides it from

> WE ALWAYS BRING ABOUT WHAT WE THINK ABOUT.

their family. It's the mask we wear to help us create an image to mislead others about who we really are and what we really want. The façade is a purposeful interruption in the byproduct process. We hold a certain belief, or we take a certain action, but we try to suppress or hide that belief or action by fabricating an alternate outcome or trying to hide it. Sooner or later, our known self emerges back onto the scene. It has to. The Known Self is the byproduct. It cannot remain covered forever. Remember, the byproduct is creating outcomes twenty-four seven at a subconscious level. In opposition, the façade is creating a mask only while consciously being applied. Sooner or later the truth, and byproduct, will emerge.

Since we are aware of this side of us but others are not, it can create outcomes which surprise us. We know what's lurking around the corners, but others may not. We see examples of the hidden self when people act out of character, only to find out later that the action or behavior which struck us as odd has existed in secret for some time. One valuable note about the hidden self as it relates to the byproduct process—We always bring about what we think about. Even though we may conceal it successfully for some time, eventually, what is inside comes out and is seen in the light of day. The byproduct of the hidden thought, belief, or desire eventually produces an outcome and can no longer be hidden.

4. **The Unknown Self** – Unknown to you and unknown to others. This is the part of us which is unknown to anyone. It may be a sort of food or music you will one day like, but you aren't currently aware you will like it. It could be

an attraction you may one day have but don't have now. It is not evident to you or to others. Since this deals primarily with the future or deeply repressed traits that never show themselves, for our conversation, we will not discuss this quadrant any further.

## THE DUNNING KRUGER EFFECT – I THINK I'M GREAT, BUT I'M NOT.

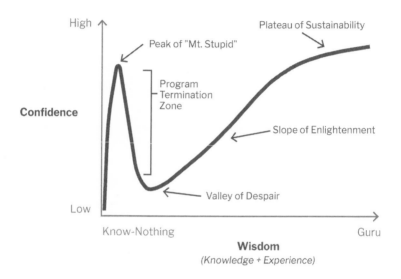

The Dunning-Kruger Effect, named after the researchers who discovered it, is one of the most interesting and commonly held delusions within our human nature. As evidenced in the graphic above, Dunning-Kruger illustrates our inability to gauge ourselves and our competency. In this study, researchers observed, quantified, and even named the human tendency to overestimate one's own competence and performance. In short, most of us believe we are better than we actually are. In one part of the study, over 80% of teachers surveyed placed themselves as above average. Almost 40% of them ranked themselves as in the top 10% of teachers. As you can see, it is impossible that 40% of teachers are in the top 10% of teachers.

This false belief ultimately leads to many false results and stops us from critically evaluating our results, beliefs, and thoughts. People who feel like they already know generally aren't concerned with learning. A great example of this effect in action is the terrible singers on American Idol. If you remember the show, half of the fun was watching these poor, tone-deaf souls pour their

> **PEOPLE WHO FEEL LIKE THEY ALREADY KNOW GENERALLY AREN'T CONCERNED WITH LEARNING.**

lives into riveting, yet wretched performances, only to be torn apart by the judges. Both they and their families were genuinely stunned by the feedback. They really believed they were good, they took action based on that belief and went on national television. That action resulted in 20 million people laughing at their self-declared talent. While most of us won't end up on national TV to be ridiculed, we are probably still overestimating our abilities. We interact with others, thinking we are better than we are, unable to recognize what is so apparent to everyone else.

As evidenced in the graphic above, most people have a tendency to feel most confident about the things they actually know the least about. Think about the aggressive alpha male who says, "I'll paint that there room", even though he has no experience in painting. At the peak of Mt. Stupid, he assumes that success will be easily achieved. However, once started down the journey, his lack of skill and expertise is met with dismal results. He has paint all over the floor, all over the trim, and all over the light switches. Very quickly, the would-be painter extraordinaire is smacked in the face with reality. This painting thing is actually a lot of work, and he doesn't know how to do it. Here, the painter enters the Valley of Despair. If he ever sees a paintbrush again…, he thinks to himself. Here, he is now aware of his lacking ability. He also has a clearer and more realistic vision of what will be required, both in effort and skill, to accomplish the completion of his project. The Valley of Despair is where most people quit most things. Those who choose to continue, now do so with a clear realization of what will be required to succeed. As they now ascend the Slope of Enlightenment, they will gain the wisdom and perspective necessary to develop their skills and complete their project. Then, finally, the painter enters the Plateau of Sustainability, where his painting skills and patience he has learned along the way become ingrained and habitual.

## THE DISC PROFILE

Another fantastic tool that helps us clearly know ourselves and others is called the DiSC Profile. I am not generally one for personality tests and assessments. They tend to be leading in the questions they ask, allowing for enormous amounts of user bias. The questions offered to determine our personality traits seem basic and polarized. Many times, the available answers are so opposite from each other, we are really picking the best of bad options to describe how we see ourselves. The DiSC profile is different. So different, in fact, that after I used it personally, I recommended all my highest producers go through the assessment as well. The data derived from this assessment is priceless for those tasked with leadership in any area. The questions used as input are variations of the same trait they are trying to identify and clarify. This forces the subject of the assessment to really think through and prioritize personal relativity on a scale from most to least. You can't simply find the best answer; you have to organize them in a hierarchy.

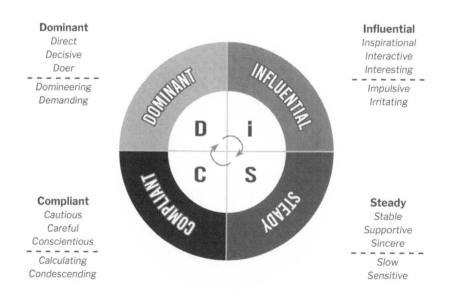

**Dominant**
*Direct*
*Decisive*
*Doer*
*Domineering*
*Demanding*

**Influential**
*Inspirational*
*Interactive*
*Interesting*
*Impulsive*
*Irritating*

**Compliant**
*Cautious*
*Careful*
*Conscientious*
*Calculating*
*Condescending*

**Steady**
*Stable*
*Supportive*
*Sincere*
*Slow*
*Sensitive*

The results were incredibly accurate for both myself and the leaders I had recommended taking the assessment. The real value is not in the identification of the "personality type." It is the inferences gained from understanding what those personality types are "like," and being able to use the DiSC database to understand the behavior and motivation spectrums of the people who possess them. The most useful of all the data points is the DiSC scatter plot, showing exactly where someone falls on the DiSC spectrum. I have included here the exact scatter plot used with my team of high achievers as an example for our upcoming discussion.

## TENDENCY: DISC EXPLAINED

Around the perimeter of the DiSC Circle are four main tendencies: Dominant, Influence, Stability, and Compliance. Within them, each of these areas contains their own batch of most commonly seen traits and tendencies. For example, Dominant tends to be very action-oriented, results focused, and low on empathy. Influence traits tend to be outgoing; they are the life of the party but may not have as high of a priority on accomplishment. Both Stability and Compliance carry their own commonalities. For a more complete list of traits and characteristics, or to complete the DiSC assessment yourself, there are many available options online for free. There are also options that, for a fee, give you more accurate, complete, and standardized assessments. In the resource section in the back of the book, I have included a link to the exact DiSC program I take my people through, complete with a discount code only available to the readers of this book! Simply visit the domain address for access to the DiSC assessment we use.

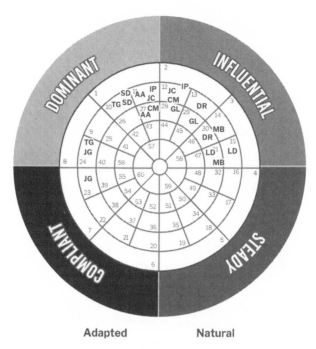

**Adapted**          **Natural**

*Initials represent individuals who were tested*

Your scatter plot will end up somewhere on the graph. The closer it is to the north, south, east, or west poles of the graph, the "more like" that you are. You will virtually always be between two poles, north and east for example. You will always be in a quadrant. That quadrant is what we would consider as your primary trait. It is possible for people to have all four traits, but most people are predominately one, with a recessive secondary trait. Let's say you are in the Dominant quadrant but closer to the Influence side than the Compliance Side. You would be considered DI or Dominant Influencer, with your primary trait as dominance, and your secondary trait as influential. If you were in the Influence quadrant closer to the Dominant side than the Stability side, you would be considered an ID, with Influence as the primary trait and Dominance as the secondary. Again, for more information on the specific traits, reference the DiSC chart above, or you can find more information by visiting the DiSC Assessment link listed on the resource page.

**Visibility of the Trait**

Once you have identified the primary and secondary traits, you will notice some respondents' points lay closer to the perimeter or outside edge of the circle, while others are more interior and closer to the center of the circle. This is the amplitude measure of the traits or how strongly those traits show themselves. If you were in the Stability quadrant and very close to the outside perimeter, you would be said to be a HIGH S. In other words, the Stability characteristics are very pronounced. They are easily observable and very forward in your personality. If you were in the Compliance quadrant, but closer towards the middle of the circle, you would be said to be a LOW C. It is still your dominating trait, but the expression of that trait is less pronounced. It isn't as easily visible or recognizable by others.

When we know where we are, we can know "how" we are, and how we function. We are able to have an accurate and clear understanding of ourselves and how we relate to the TBAR process. We are less likely to create or trust faulty input into the TBAR process, which in turn makes us less likely to create outcomes we weren't expecting or desiring.

# NATURAL VS. ADAPTED STYLE

In my opinion, the most valuable part of the DiSC assessment is the delineation and explanation of a natural style and adapted style. As you can see on the scatterplot, all respondents actually have two points on the graph. One is the placement of the respondent's natural style; the other is the placement of the adapted style.

### The Natural Style

The natural style is who you are. It's your natural response and tendency. It's your hardwired personality, evident for all to see.

### The Adapted Style

The adapted style is best understood as your learned personality, the person you have created out of a need to fit in or for acceptance or economic survival. It is not your naturally occurring self, but the self you have created to socialize and function in society.

The natural style is the result of your naturally occurring byproduct process. Your adapted style is a form of created TBAR process. When natural and adapted styles are far away from each other on the graph, there is tension and distance between who we are and who we think we should be. This tension causes enormous amounts of inner turmoil and leads to decreased performance and lower overall happiness and well-being. People whose natural and adapted styles are closer together on the graph are in more alignment. Who they really are, and who they believe they need to be, are very close to each other. They are able to move through life authentically and don't suffer from the problems misalignment brings. The closer our natural and adapted styles are, the more ingrained the byproduct process has become. The adapted style has moved to a subconscious belief system that is nearly identical to the natural style belief system. The further the two points are away from each other, the less ingrained the byproduct process is. The adapted style, or who we think we need to be, is still at the conscious level. *I know I need to be or do more of X to accomplish what I'm aiming for.* Maybe this is a conscious thought, but it is not operating at the subconscious level yet. Once the adapted style joins the natural style, operating at the subconscious level, they actually

> **THE CLOSER OUR NATURAL AND ADAPTED STYLES ARE, THE MORE INGRAINED THE BYPRODUCT PROCESS HAS BECOME.**

have a gravitational effect and pull the natural and adapted styles closer to one another. This, in turn, creates a more aligned, unified person. Your natural style can and will be influenced by a highly expressive adapted style. The creation of an adapted style occurs through the TBAR process and can largely be directed and cultivated.

One of the underlying commonalities amongst high achievers is that there is very little difference between their natural and adapted style. In other words, their actual self, who they actually are and what they actually believe, and their adapted style, which is the person they feel they must be in order to succeed, are extremely similar. The greatest leaders in all areas almost always have very little distinction between the two. Who they are and who they feel they need to be are the same. They are able to run unhindered in the direction of their pursuits without interference from cognitive dissonance or the difference between what they believe and what they are doing.

When what we say we want and what we actually want are too far apart, the cognitive dissonance eventually becomes so large that it stops us from pursuing our goal any further.

As a side note, different areas of expertise and results require different strengths on the DiSC profile. There are no right and wrong tendencies, just tendencies that lead to great results in different areas. For example, an outstanding accountant probably has a high degree of compliance in their natural and adapted styles to keep track of the countless and ever-changing rules in the accounting field. A YouTube star, on the other hand, may need zero compliance to be successful but requires a high amount of influence to DOMINATE IN THEIR FIELD. There is no right and wrong, only information to be used.

When we have a clear understanding of who we are and how we are, we can begin to understand our tendencies. Self-mastery is one of the common traits of all high achievers. In the coming chapters, we will explore even further into who we are and why we act the way we act. When we REALLY know who we are and why we do the things we do, we can use the BYPRODUCT process quickly and efficiently to change our lives.

# 6

# HOW WE LOSE

**W**ell-managed loss is one of the most common causes of success. Mismanaged success is one of the most common causes of loss. One of the most important things we can learn about ourselves is how we handle losing. Contrary to what the general public is taught in schools, losing is not bad. It's necessary. Anybody who has ever achieved anything worthwhile knows that losing is part of the process on the road to success. The difference between winners and losers is this—Losers let the loss define them, winners let the loss refine them. Like it or not, we are all going to face our share of losses along our journey. Deciding upfront how we are going to process those losses and what we will take from them when they do occur plays a huge role in our ability to use the TBAR process effectively.

> **WELL-MANAGED LOSS IS ONE OF THE MOST COMMON CAUSES OF SUCCESS.**

American evangelist, publisher, and founder of Moody Bible Institute D.L. Moody said in a sermon about failure: "Our greatest fear should not be of failure, but of succeeding at something that doesn't really matter." Without ample doses of failure, our lives are at risk of insignificance.

How we handle loss has a lot to do with what we believe about losing. There are two distinctive belief systems when it comes to understanding and processing defeat. They are the confirmation belief system and the opportunity belief system. The confirmation belief system interprets loss as a confirmation of existing doubts and limiting beliefs. When we experience a loss under this mindset, we think things like, "I'm not any good at sales," "I need to stay with what I know," "I'm just not cut out for this." The truth is, you are cut out for whatever you want to be cut out for. The

> **ANYBODY WHO HAS EVER ACHIEVED ANYTHING WORTHWHILE KNOWS THAT LOSING IS PART OF THE PROCESS ON THE ROAD TO SUCCESS.**

opportunity mindset says, "That didn't go how I expected, what can I learn from this that will make me better and help me avoid this again in the future?" People with this belief system look at losses and setbacks as opportunities to refine and develop their skills and eliminate weakness, which will ultimately get them closer to their goal.

## DON'T JUST LOSE, GET THE LESSON

As Chris Brady and Orrin Woodward discuss in their book *Launching a Leadership Revolution*, every loss brings with it two benefits:

1. Data

2. Pressure

Inside every loss is a reason for the loss and a lesson to be learned. "Why did I lose?" is the question every great champion asks themselves when faced with setbacks or adversity. They don't scapegoat or make excuses, they don't blame

> **LOSERS LET THE LOSS DEFINE THEM, WINNERS LET THE LOSS REFINE THEM.**

the coach or the refs or their teammates, they own it. They think *I've already paid a price by losing. I'm going to extract whatever benefit I can from this, so*

*I don't lose again.* Embedded in every loss is wrong thinking, wrong believing, or wrong action. A great performer hunts down the truth and shores up their weaknesses, becoming an even more formidable competitor in the process.

The pressure of the loss is where true greats are born. You either hate losing enough to change, or you hate changing enough to lose. When someone is repeatedly stopped short of their goal (a loss), a positive pressure begins to

> **THE TRUTH IS, YOU ARE CUT OUT FOR WHATEVER YOU WANT TO BE CUT OUT FOR.**

build. With every loss along the way, the pressure increases and grows until it finally bursts. The competitor becomes willing to think, believe, and act in ways they previously were unwilling to. They use the pressure of the loss to create the pain needed to change. Greats don't waste pain; they use it. Most of us, however, have not created the opportunity belief system in our lives, so we spend most of our time avoiding the loss or minimizing it when it happens instead of learning and growing through it. There are two types of losers who hold to the confirmation mindset, and we will examine them both.

**Loss Avoiders**

Losing hurts. When we don't have the proper belief system in place saying to us, "Although painful, this will ultimately help me," we will go to great lengths to avoid being in a losing situation. We begin to play it safe. We play not to lose, instead of playing to win. We don't venture outside our comfort zone. We will remove ourselves from any situation where we might be faced with a loss or the fact that we aren't good enough. We go to great lengths to stay in our lane.

> **YOU EITHER HATE LOSING ENOUGH TO CHANGE, OR YOU HATE CHANGING ENOUGH TO LOSE.**

Loss avoiders never really go all in because they're afraid of being defined by what's on the other side. Avoiders tend to react to the possibility of loss by removing themselves from it.

I am an avoider. The best story I can share with you to illustrate this is from my childhood as a star in the city sandlot leagues. My team was in game three of a three-game World Series against our crosstown rivals. I was known around the league as one of the the best pitchers along with my friend and competitor on the other team.

Tied one game to one, it was winner takes all. Up 2-0 for the first four

**GREATS DON'T WASTE PAIN; THEY USE IT.**

of seven innings, we were the home team. At the top of the fourth, I walked a batter and then got two outs. Trying to put it away for the inning, the next batter lined into center field for a single, putting a runner on first and third. The next pitch, the runner stole second. Then the unthinkable, another walk. Bases loaded, the go-ahead run on first, and it was too much for me to bear. I called the coach out to the mound and gave him the ball. I asked him to take me out of the game. I claimed my arm was in excruciating pain from the last pitch. The truth is, I was scared. I was scared everyone would see I wasn't as good as they thought I was, and I wasn't as good as I thought I was. I took myself out of the game and watched from the sidelines. Instead of facing what was on the other side of the next batter, I sat myself on the bench. This is exactly what avoiders do—they bench themselves in the game of life. That moment has haunted me for twenty-five years; it's something I keep with me to this day. *What would have happened?* In the high-pressure moments, the greats call for the ball. I should have stayed in, but I didn't. When I'm faced with a negative situation in the future, I remember the pain of regret and tell myself to get on the field and to take a swing.

### Minimizers

Minimizers are people who downplay the win so they don't feel bad about losing. "I didn't really want that thing anyway", "There is more to life than _____." These

people are always quick to rain on other people's parades, trying to

**THIS IS EXACTLY WHAT AVOIDERS DO—THEY BENCH THEMSELVES IN THE GAME OF LIFE.**

convince themselves and others of the validity of their lack of engagement. "Who needs a house like that anyway?" "Why would someone ever want that kind of car? It probably gets really bad gas mileage", "Don't work so hard; you can't take it with you!" And when their family breaks up, the minimizer says, "As long as I'm happy, that's what matters." They excuse their loss by devaluing the win.

PRESSURE squeezes effort out of winners and excuses out of losers!

Which one are you? Inside virtually all of us, there is an avoider or minimizer lurking, attempting to steal the wisdom gained from losing and discouraging us from continuing into greatness. These are incorrect beliefs. Being aware of your tendency will help you recognize these beliefs and damaging self-talk

> **PRESSURE SQUEEZES EFFORT OUT OF WINNERS AND EXCUSES OUT OF LOSERS!**

when they surface. At this point, you now have the awareness and the tools set to recognize, replace, and reprogram a better series of thoughts and beliefs so that when losses occur what would have stopped most people, you turn into fuel. Just by knowing which you are, you are able to recognize when you are using avoidance or minimizing to excuse yourself from the game of life.

# 7

# HOW WE WIN

## THE THREE LEVELS OF MOTIVATION

A fter a discussion about appropriately handling failure and how it relates to the TBAR process, we should have a brief discussion on how we win and the three levels of motivation. Addressed further in the "Action" section of the book, here is a brief synopsis of the three levels of motivation, and how we use them in alignment with the TBAR process. This concept of the levels of motivation was originally discussed in the book *Launching a Leadership Revolution* by Chris Brady and Orrin Woodward. In the book, they discuss three ascending levels of motivation, starting at the most basic and moving towards the most complex. Here, we will understand them and apply them to the use of the TBAR process.

1. **Level One – Material Motivation.** Material motivation is the most basic human motivation. The need for food, shelter, clothing, and other basic material needs provides motivation to us every day. Each day, hundreds of millions of people leave their families and head to jobs they don't like to spend the best years of their lives attempting to meet these basic material needs.

"I'm not money motivated," is the cry from the perpetually low on money. Let's hear that again when someone loses their job and is in danger of losing their home, car, etc. The truth is that we are all materially motivated. Material motivation is a great tool encouraging us to provide value and service to others in return for meeting our material needs. Used appropriately, material motivation has the capability of greatly increasing your productivity and level of your results.

**The power of equilibrium and material motivation**

### EQUILIBRIUM

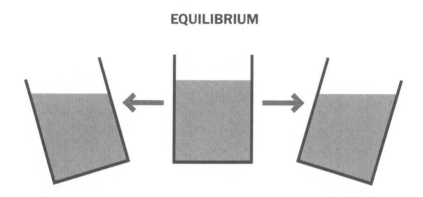

Let's discuss the concept of equilibrium. It is the most natural state of any matter or cell. Picture a bottle of water half full. Turn the bottle slightly sideways. What happens to the water inside? The water literally repositions itself to be level to the earth even though its container has shifted. It is searching for equilibrium. We operate in much the same way. We live in a certain size house, have certain types of cars, and are accustomed to certain standards of living. Take these things away through a job loss or some other interruption of the quality of life, and we become highly motivated to maintain this standard or state of equilibrium. We will change companies, move our families, or learn new skills, all to maintain equilibrium. This is an incredibly useful survival mechanism. Equilibrium is also in and of itself a byproduct. All those outcomes, the car, the house, the lifestyle, are byproducts of the thinking, belief, and actions we have taken. The cycle repeats itself, and if interrupted, equilibrium attempts to bring us right back to the same state as before.

Understanding this, great achievers have used material motivation for incredible leverage through reprogramming. If your lifestyle equilibrium is set at $150,000 annually, you could reprogram it to $300,000 annually by surrounding yourself with the outcomes of such a lifestyle. Go visit a model home that's two to three times the size of your current home, go drive your dream car and ask yourself one question: "How do I get these things?" The answer to this question serves as the starting input or thought in a new TBAR process. When you surround yourself with different outcomes, you expose yourself to the thinking which created them. You are creating different inputs which will eventually create different outcomes.

### The Stick and the Carrot

While having a discussion on the material level of motivation, I would be remiss to pass over a conversation about the stick and the carrot. When it comes to material motivation, there are two types of people—stick people and carrot people. Stick people are primarily motivated by the avoidance of pain. Their actions are generally in response to some anticipated pain and avoiding it. They learn a new skill, so they don't lose the job, they are behind on the car payment so they look for additional work. They respond to and move away from negative material outcomes. Carrot people are the opposite of stick people. They are motivated by the prize, the

> **WHEN YOU SURROUND YOURSELF WITH DIFFERENT OUTCOMES, YOU EXPOSE YOURSELF TO THE THINKING WHICH CREATED THEM.**

potential, and the possibilities. The big house, the nice car, and the fancy watch motivate them to earn. The hard body, the way they look in the swimsuit, motivate them to work out.

There is no right and wrong, just an understanding of who you are and how you work. If you are a carrot person, tie your goals to a reward. The reward adds extra gravity to believe the work will be worth the reward. If you are a stick person, create a false pain. Do not wait to hit hard times for motivation; create faux pain instead.

Either way, stick or carrot, the more you know about yourself and how you use and respond to motivation, the more you can use the techniques to supercharge the TBAR process in your life. The problem with material motivations is it's the shallowest level of motivation available. Not a moral shallowness, but shallow in the meaning that once the thing motivating you has been obtained, it no longer motivates you. Once you have the dream car, it ceases to exert motivational pressure on you.

2. **Level Two – Respect and Recognition.** Operating at a much deeper level of human nature, the attainment of respect and recognition from peers and mentors is a much longer lasting and more meaningful type of motivation. Everybody wants to be somebody. Everyone wants praise and recognition, and once we attain it, we will go to great lengths to keep it. It exudes pressure on us to keep succeeding after we have had initial levels of success.

3. **Level Three – Legacy and Purpose.** At this level of motivation, the conversation shifts from us and our lives, to the impact we will have beyond our lifetime. What will my life mean? How will I be remembered? What sort of impact will I leave on the planet? People operating at this level of motivation have the ability to run a continual cycle of growth and improvement through their entire lifetimes and achieve monumental heights in their fields. They never shut down the purposeful TBAR process in their lives.

More discussion on the three levels of motivation will happen later in the book. Right now, we want to focus on how knowing ourselves becomes a tool to assist the TBAR and byproduct processes. It does this by providing the best and most accurate information about ourselves, our thinking, and beliefs.

These are all tools we can use to help insulate the byproduct process from the attack of emotions, feelings, and failure mechanisms. When we know who we are and how we are, we can move through the TBAR process with awareness of the potential pitfalls along the way. **Once you know how TBAR works and how you work, we are ready to explore each component piece to optimize your results.**

# SECTION THREE
# THOUGHT

# 8

## THOUGHTS ARE THINGS

### ALL PHYSICAL THINGS HAVE BEEN CREATED TWICE, FIRST IN THE MIND OF MAN, THEN IN REALITY.

T he most explosive times of growth in leadership come when the thinking which brought us to where we are fundamentally changes into the thinking that will get us where we are going. Remember, where you are RIGHT NOW is the exact byproduct of your thinking, beliefs, and actions. When the fundamental thinking undergoes a major shift, all the other factors will undergo fundamental change as well automatically, given time. While most people never think about what

> ### WE LIVE LIFE BY DEFAULT OR DESIGN, AND GREAT LEADERS ARE ALWAYS THE ARCHITECTS OF THEIR LIVES.

they are thinking about, a leader knows one of their most important roles is to take ownership in directing their thinking. We live life by default or design, and great leaders are always the architects of their lives.

### WHAT IS THOUGHT?

You can't WIN in life when you are LOSING in your mind. To better understand the power of our thoughts, let's look at the mechanics of how they are formed.

In his book *Think and Grow Rich*, Napoleon Hill made the statement, "Thoughts are things." When we have a thought, a sequence of neurons fire which are unique to the thought. When those neurons fire, in addition to the thought, there are certain chemical reactions happening in the brain associated with that specific thought. The more a thought repeats, the more easily the neurons fire, and the more of the chemical sequence is released. Over time, a neural pathway is formed, making it easier and easier to repeat that thought process until the pathway is so well worn, it becomes difficult to change. That thought is now well worn and heavily ingrained and becomes a building block of belief. A thought repeated often enough, whether true or not, becomes part of a belief. We will deal with beliefs in the next chapter, so for now, let's focus on the thought.

> A THOUGHT REPEATED OFTEN ENOUGH, WHETHER TRUE OR NOT, BECOMES PART OF A BELIEF.

In his book *Breaking the Habit of Becoming Yourself*, Dr. Joe Dispenza discusses how the chemical reactions of each thought, over time, actually create addictions in the brain. When thought "A" occurs, it releases a chemical cocktail specific to that thought. Think thought "A" often enough, and the brain actually becomes addicted to it. It craves the chemicals created by thought "A" and yearns for it to repeat over and over. We actually become physically addicted to our current thought processes. In other words, the more we think a thought, the more our brain becomes chemically dependent on the release of this specific chemical formula. When we try to change our thinking and thought processes, the brain actually goes through a sort of withdrawal and tries to meet its need by firing the existing thought autonomously from the subconscious level. Is it any wonder it is difficult to change our thinking when we are literally addicted to being ourselves?

## AS A MAN THINKETH, SO IS HE

We are constantly moving in the direction of our most dominant thought. Over time, the most dominant thought moves its way from the conscious to the subconscious and becomes part of the fabric of our operating system; our beliefs. It begins to work autonomously of your conscious effort. Twenty-four hours a day, seven days a week, that thought, which became a belief, is creating a byproduct in the actions or inactions you are taking on a daily basis. Our thinking is always creating, adding to, or changing our beliefs. Our beliefs are constantly creating our actions, and our actions are creating our results. The thought is the origin of all accomplishment and all failure. It would make sense that we would spend time and effort to understand WHAT we are thinking and to evaluate WHY WE ARE THINKING IT. It is also useful to understand WHETHER OR NOT THAT THOUGHT IS ACCURATE. Remember, a thought doesn't need to be true to create corresponding beliefs, actions, and results; it must only be thought often enough.

## THINK BIG – BIG GOALS CREATE BIG RESULTS

Even if we don't accomplish them at first, setting a big goal and missing it is better than succeeding at a smaller one. We are thinking all the time anyways, why not guide our thinking in the direction we want our lives to take and THINK BIG! Most of us see only what's right in front of us and scale our lives back to fit into the box of our current existence. Our thinking and our vision are influenced by our surroundings, our peers, and our status quo. Stop for a second and think about what you really want. If money and time were no issue, what would you be doing with your days? Where would you travel? What would you do for and with the people you love most? What impact projects would you be working on? What difference would you like to make in the world? Now, think on those things. Spend time reviewing them, writing them, visualizing them. Your thoughts start the byproduct reaction in your life. The better quality the thought, the better quality the outcome. One of my all-time favorite quotes, attributed to Sir Francis Drake, says this about thinking small:

"Disturb us, Lord, when
We are too pleased with ourselves,
When our dreams have come true
Because we dreamed too little,

When we arrived safely
Because we sailed too close to the shore."

It costs nothing to think big, so stretch your vision, get around people and go to places out of your norm. Be around those who represent who and where you want to be. Think on these things.

Think about our thoughts in this way. While they are all creating a byproduct belief, they also act like gravity. The larger the mass, the more the gravitational force associated with it. In other words, the bigger the object, the more pull it has on things. Thoughts are the same way. The bigger the thought, the larger pull it has on your life and the byproduct process. Thinking big has the power to captivate the soul and add firepower to the beliefs which will be developed through the byproduct process.

# 9

# GOALS DON'T WORK

## GOALS - THOUGHTS WITH A TIMETABLE

G oals are really nothing more than thoughts about how we want things to be, attached to a timetable for achieving them. But what do we do when we don't hit our goals? The honest truth is, sooner or later, consistently missing goals is what stops people on the path to their dreams. When we don't hit goals, it's for one of three reasons.

One: It wasn't our goal.
We never owned it. We liked the idea of the goal but lacked the emotional buy-in required to see it through to the completion phase. These are sometimes other's goals for us which we try to adopt as our own. Before you get too excited

> GREAT LEADERS ARE FIRST GREAT FOLLOWERS.

and say, "See that's why I don't hit my goals... they aren't really my goals," remember—we are responsible to adopt our leader's goals and our team's goals as our own. Great leaders are first great followers. Before you build a team, you will be part of a team. Leaders learn how to make the team's goals their goals. It is our responsibility. As my good friend and entrepreneur Joseph Ward says, "Most people lie about their why." He's saying most people's stated goals and dreams really aren't their goals and dreams. Stated goal: "I want to help the starving kids around the world." If you really cared about the starving kids, you wouldn't need someone to pump you up about crushing your goals! The missed goal might be what you believe *should* be your goal or what may sound good to

> **MANY GOALS ARE REALLY JUST WISHES.**

other people. Your goals don't need to be altruistic; they just need to be real. What do you REALLY want? Remember, goals and dreams are really just thoughts with a deadline. Since THOUGHTS always produce the byproduct of belief, action, and results, when we lack sufficient action towards our stated goal, we can assume there is little authenticity about the goal.

Two: The skills aren't developed.
Many goals are really just wishes. They are fantasy where we envision ourselves or our team creating outcomes which our skill sets don't allow us to achieve. For example, you may have a goal of being a Major League Baseball player. But if you don't practice and train to prepare for it, the goal won't become reality, no matter how bad you want it to. Our goals must be congruent with our skill sets. When they are not, we have two choices, reduce our goals or grow our skill set.

Three: Delusion.
Delusion is the gap between what we believe it should take and what it actually takes. Many people believe accomplishing their goals will be easier and take less time than it actually will. They believe this because they lack the ability to accurately assess cause and effect. When they are finally confronted with the volume of effort required, over a much longer period of time than they initially believed, most

> **OUR GOALS MUST BE CONGRUENT WITH OUR SKILL SETS. WHEN THEY ARE NOT, WE HAVE TWO CHOICES, REDUCE OUR GOALS OR GROW OUR SKILL SET.**

people abandon ship. This is where champions dig in deeper, knowing most of their competition has given up, and now is the time to strike. Achieving your goal demands the price be paid up front and in full. We never adjust our goal down; we take our effort up. When the only misalignment is effort, we always put in more effort. Hitting your goal is like walking up a downward escalator. There are only two places you can stop—at the bottom or at the top. If we stop halfway to the goal, we eventually end up right back where we began. We must see it to completion, even if we have to skill up and double down on our efforts.

## INPUT GOALS VS. OUTPUT GOALS

By definition, goals are thoughts about a desired outcome in a desired time frame. They provide great raw material to create empowering and productive beliefs, yet most people who set goals fail to hit those goals on a consistent basis. Every January, people join gyms like crazy, eat right, and head in the direction of losing weight. Yet by mid-February, most of these goals are off track, and great intentions have gone by the wayside. Why? The goal was an output goal. In other words, it was

> HITTING YOUR GOAL IS LIKE WALKING UP A DOWNWARD ESCALATOR. THERE ARE ONLY TWO PLACES YOU CAN STOP—AT THE BOTTOM OR AT THE TOP.

a goal focused on the result. While these goals are extremely important in directing our thoughts, beliefs, and actions, they hold little power to help us traverse the distance between our current reality and the reality we desire. Why? Because we are focused on the byproduct instead of the input.

Because every outcome is the perfect byproduct of its input, it would make sense to create input-based goals. These are goals based on achieving component pieces of the overall goal. Succeed at reaching those and, by default, create the outcome you desire.

For example, someone might have a goal of losing ten pounds in six weeks. It's a fantastic goal and provides great direction and the input for the byproduct process to start with. But a better goal may be to go to the gym four times a week and eat less than 2500 calories a day. The byproduct of those inputs will create the weight loss desired and are trackable and achievable on a daily basis. By breaking large outcomes into the pieces which will construct them, we can get more immediate and accurate feedback on our progress. In this example, we receive feedback on a daily basis from our calorie intake. We also receive feedback on a weekly basis from our gym attendance. Tracking these inputs provides faster and more reliable feedback than waiting for six weeks to see if we lost the ten pounds.

> **WHAT YOU ARE USING AS AN EXCUSE, SOMEONE ELSE IS USING AS MOTIVATION. NEVER FORGET IT.**

The problem with outcome goals is that we have to wait to see if they have been achieved. By the time we miss them, there's nothing we can do about it. We can track and assess input goals as we are doing them and use them as course corrections.

When we create input goals, we succeed at creating the next domino in the chain reaction of cause and effect. If our goal is to lose ten pounds in six weeks but don't create input goals, we run the risk of taking no action or too little action. When we create component input goals, the pieces of the larger goal, we can take immediate action. When our goal is to go to the gym four times this week, we can measure that input goal four times this week versus the zero times we would be able to measure the goal of losing ten pounds in six weeks. This can be applied in literally every area of life. In sales, an output goal might be to do a million dollars in

> **EXCUSES ARE THE GRAVEYARD OF DREAMS AND THE FLOWERBED OF DISAPPOINTMENT.**

revenue this year. An input goal tied to this might be to make fifteen calls a day all year to hit the million dollars in revenue. It will take us the full year to truly measure the output goal, but we can measure the input goal every day.

I can't talk about goals without hitting a common response when a goal goes unmet: Excuses.

People who are good at making excuses are seldom good at anything else. What you are using as an EXCUSE, someone else is using as MOTIVATION. Never forget it.

Excuses are thoughts used to rationalize a loss. Today's culture is saturated with excuses. The reality is—you didn't get it done. Period. Excuses are the graveyard of dreams and the flowerbed of disappointment. You can make excuses or money, but you can't make both. An excuse is a thought which attempts to delineate the cause and effect relationship. It helps us to remove the pain of failure by attempting to remove our responsibility in the creation of our own outcome. You want to stand out amongst the crowd? Become a person who neither gives, nor accepts excuses. You will make yourself, and everyone else around you, better. This is a NO EXCUSES ZONE.

# 10

# SYSTEM UPGRADE

## SHIFT THE OUTCOME - HOW TO MAKE THE CHANGE

As discussed earlier in the book, when we have incorrect thinking or beliefs, we take incorrect action and get incorrect results. How do we know we are having incorrect results? Our results are not what we want or desire or they create pain in our lives or the lives of others. Our ability to identify poor results (thinking) is the start of change. We need to be able to call a "spade a spade." Today, everyone gets a trophy, but that's not how the world works. If you don't like the

> **SUCCESS LEAVES CLUES.**

results you're getting, then get better. Poor health, lack of financial resources, and struggling to maintain meaningful relationships are just a few of the indicators we may be failing to connect the dots in our lives.

What's causing the negatives in your life?

Are you sure?

What's causing the positives in your life?

Are you sure?

What are all of the things that are going well?

Are you sure?

What causes people to become wealthy? Luck? Right place at the right time? Or was it the creation of a product, service, or idea that filled a need and was easily distributed to the masses? Maybe it was attaining a highly specialized skill set which very few possess but many demand? Could it be that it was using money to buy assets instead of liabilities? Are you able to see the cause and effect?

When we chalk success up to luck, we chalk our lives up to mediocrity.

Awareness of cause and effect allows us to use cause and effect to create what we desire in life. The inability to see cause and effect stops us from using this most incredible process and leaves us perpetually clueless, waiting on the savior politician to deliver us from ourselves. You can use this question exercise with almost any outcome you wish to attain. How do people lose weight? How do they have such a great marriage? How could I accomplish this or that? Discovering cause and effect is the key. Choose the right input and the byproduct process changes your life.

The process for creating a different thought pattern starts with the awareness that the current thought pattern isn't yielding the right results. It is the recognition that your thinking, and not something in the outside world, is creating your outcome. Knowing this truth puts you much farther down the road of success and excellence than most of the rest of the world.

Once we have identified our thoughts aren't serving us, the best place to find the thoughts which will serve us is through the people who have the results we want. Tried and true leaders in any field think differently, and if you are observant, the differences between their thinking and yours will become apparent very quickly. Because results are always the byproduct of the TBAR process, correct results over long periods of time are the natural byproduct of a true and accurate thought process. Dig deep into their material. All the books on success have already been written (officially now with the release of *BYPRODUCT*). There just aren't

86

enough readers. Books, podcasts, and videos from the people whose results we would like to emulate help us to discern the differences between their thinking and ours. Success leaves clues. What is different about their speech, behavior, and reactions? How do they treat people? If possible, ask them directly what they did to achieve those results or what their thoughts are about a certain aspect of life. Study those with right results, get their thinking, and create replacement thoughts for your own.

## UPGRADE YOUR OPERATING SYSTEM

As discussed earlier in the book, the first step to lasting change is the recognition, replacement, and reprogramming of less optimal thoughts and thought processes with better and more accurate thinking. This is done through what I call *replace and reprogram*, similar to what Napoleon Hill calls the *principle of auto-suggestion*.

Remember, the subconscious mind doesn't reason. It doesn't evaluate truth or falsehood; it simply accepts what you give it. The process of giving it new information happens through replacing and reprogramming the desired thought until it breaks through the subconscious veil. Good or bad, helpful or harmful, any thought repeated often and vividly enough will eventually make its way into the subconscious and become part of your operating system, where it is accepted as true and begins to form its own byproduct, BELIEF.

The Process for Reprogramming

To begin the process of reprogramming your thinking, you must follow these steps:

1. Identify the thought you wish to replace.

2. Create a new, more accurate thought (thought reframing).

3. Verbalize it and write it in the present tense.

4. Repeat it as many times a day as possible.

5. Record a self-talk audio to be able to listen to the statements in your own voice.

Over time, this constant repetition will take the thought passed the gatekeeper of the conscious mind and lodge it firmly in the subconscious.

Remember, the new statement doesn't have to be true to be eventually accepted and then formed as a belief. Most of what we currently believe is inaccurate as evidenced by our limited results, yet we believe it and act on those beliefs every single day. As you begin to craft new thoughts, don't concern yourself about whether the replacement thoughts are true for you, they just must be true in general. For example, you may have a statement such as, "I am my ideal weight and I feel great about how I look," even though right now you don't feel great about how you look. When you are your ideal weight, will you feel great about how you look? ABSOLUTELY! Therefore, the thought is TRUE. It just isn't a current reality for you yet. It is important we create the new thoughts in light of the truth, because truth always produces the right results. If outcomes are the byproduct, traced all the way back to the thoughts we think, it is precisely that nobody is thinking about what they are thinking about, that is the cause of mass mediocrity.

## REFRAMING OUR THOUGHTS FOR OPTIMAL RESULTS

Reframing is how we create our new thoughts. It's simply a shift in thinking from a current negative, to a future positive. For example, it's taking the thought, *I'm overweight, to, I am adopting a lifestyle to achieve my ideal weight. From, I don't like this person, to, I am finding the qualities which make them likeable. It's moving from, I can't afford it, to, How can I afford it?*

When we move from fatalistic thoughts to a reframed, ownership outlook thought process, it opens our thinking to solutions. For example, when we say, "I can't afford it," the byproduct is a belief which says don't worry about trying to find a solution. When we think, *How can I afford it?*, our mind becomes infinitely creative, looking for the solution to the problem at hand. When we begin to look for solutions, we develop the BELIEF that a solution is possible. This belief creates action in the direction of finding the solution. Enough action in that direction ultimately will produce greater results than when the brain shuts down and does not accept responsibility for the solution.

It also helps to get around people who can reinforce the right thinking. The reason most people don't believe they will achieve their goals is that they hang out with people who have already given up on theirs.

The reason most people don't think they can make 75-100k a *month* is because they surround themselves with people who are making 75-100k a *year*.

The reason most people don't believe they can lose weight and look great is because they hang with people who stopped caring about their health a long time ago.

What's the moral? Get around people who are headed in the same direction as you.

We must think about what we think about, evaluate the root thoughts through the lens of the outcomes they produce, seek out better thoughts from those further than us, and use the replace and reprogram process to change our thinking for massive success! Once our purposely directed thoughts become part of our subconscious, they begin to weave into the fabric of our beliefs. We will discuss this in the next section.

# SECTION FOUR
## BELIEFS

# 11

# THE THERMOSTAT

**BELIEFS ARE POWERFUL THINGS, THEY PUT A MAN ON THE MOON, AND THEY BRING ABOUT A MAN'S DARKEST HOUR.**

B elief is the thermostat that regulates what we accomplish in life. WE ACT ON BELIEFS, PERIOD.

The belief all men are created equal and have certain unalienable rights, bestowed on them by the creator of the universe caused Thomas Jefferson and the American colonies to declare independence from Great Britain and to create a government of the people, by the people, and for the people. The belief that all men are not created equal and that some races should dominate over others, created the rise of Adolf Hitler. Both actions mark the history of mankind, and both were byproducts of beliefs.

Believe you are just big boned, you probably won't start a diet. Believe you are destined for greatness in business, you will probably start

**BELIEF IS THE THERMOSTAT THAT REGULATES WHAT WE ACCOMPLISH IN LIFE.**

several businesses looking for your breakthrough. Our beliefs direct our course of action and ultimately the outcome of our lives, so we better make sure they are accurate and are serving us.

History is full of people who truly believed something that just wasn't true. Their belief turned into an action (sometimes an inaction), and the byproduct of that action resulted. Likewise, our lives are full of "should have been, could have been, and would have been" people who were a few small belief upgrades away from being total world changers.

It does not matter what happens to you, what matters is how you respond. The BELIEF SYSTEM is the lens through which we view all of life's experiences. For example, two students fail their algebra exam. One has a belief system says which anything is learnable with enough time and effort. The belief system where success is eventual if the right effort and study time is put in, makes a student much more likely to view the failure as temporary. It's also likely to drive them to study harder and longer, looking for ways to improve their math skills. The other student has the belief that they

> **IT DOES NOT MATTER WHAT HAPPENS TO YOU, WHAT MATTERS IS HOW YOU RESPOND.**

just aren't a very good student, and this probably isn't going to change. This student's motivation level to seek help and put in extra effort is greatly reduced compared to that of the student with the other belief system. The above example is a play-out of the battle between the opportunity mindset and the confirmation mindsets discussed earlier in the book. While there are ultimately unlimited numbers of beliefs and belief systems, virtually all beliefs fit into one of these two categories: confirmation belief or opportunity belief.

Another way to think of a belief is as a world view, a lens through which we interpret what happens to us or around us and helps us assign meaning and understanding in our life. Beliefs, many times, represent a synthesis of several thoughts or ideas working together. For example, a thought might be: *I don't know how that person became so successful.* Another thought is, *I'm not as successful as they are.* Another may be, *I work as hard as they do.* The belief synthesized from these thoughts may form along these lines: *Since I view myself as working as hard or harder than them, but I'm not as successful as they are, and since I don't understand how their success was created, I develop the belief their success, or maybe even success in general, is based on luck or something special they possess that I don't.* In this example, the belief creates inaction towards taking steps to improve and prepare for future success ahead. Because you don't believe it has much to do with you or that you can create the desired outcome, you don't even bother to try.

Our beliefs color how we interpret the circumstances we are in and the events happening around us. During a presidential debate, two people with different political belief systems will listen to the exact same dialogue but come to drastically different conclusions about what was said and who was right. It's an identical stimulus but reacted to and acted upon in two very different ways. Because our actions are always a byproduct of our beliefs, it's important to make sure our beliefs are accurate.

Let's examine four universes of belief.

1. **Erroneous beliefs** are beliefs founded on incorrect thoughts or assumptions.

2. **Limiting beliefs** are beliefs rooted in doubt, they can be erroneous or based in truth, but with limited perspective applied to them.

3. **Empowering beliefs** are beliefs based in truth and rooted in cause and effect.

4. **Standards** are what we expect out of life.


### Erroneous Beliefs

False beliefs create poor outcomes. For instance, let's examine a common belief which results in a lack of resources for enormous amounts of people.

Belief: Rich people are greedy, bad, or having money isn't good. God doesn't want us to have too much money.

Examination of belief: Are there wealthy people who do good, positive, and productive things with their money? Yes.

If there are wealthy people who use their resources as a service to others, then the belief that rich people are greedy or bad is untrue, at least as a blanket statement. Some may be, but the blanket belief where having too much money is bad or will make you greedy is clearly incorrect. If we base our approach to money upon these false beliefs, is it any wonder why we struggle financially?

God has NO PROBLEM with you having money, just as long as money doesn't have you. Just look at Abraham, Solomon, David, Job, all regarded as among the wealthiest men of their time, and all used by God in a mighty way.

Incorrect as it may be, someone holding this belief is eventually going to reap its byproduct—a lack of money. When you believe money is bad or evil, you won't take action to acquire it. A lack of money in the lives of hundreds of millions of people in North America isn't a lack of skill or opportunity, but a byproduct of a belief which says we shouldn't desire money. Let's take a look at the creation of the byproduct.

Incorrect belief: People who have money are greedy. I'm not greedy, I don't want to be greedy, so I better be careful about accumulating money.

Corresponding action: Disinterest in opportunities to make and accumulate money. Disinterest in learning about and applying financial principles or becoming educated about money and finance

Corresponding result: Low income, little or no money saved, accumulation of debt.

We will always act on our belief whether the belief is true or false. True beliefs come from accurate thinking. False beliefs come from inaccurate thinking.

**Examples of Erroneous Beliefs:**

**Success is a result of luck.**
**I am unlucky.**
**Successful people are special or different than I am.**
**I am just wired this way.**
**According to my astrological sign...**
**My circumstances are unique to me.**
**No one else has the problems I have.**

Losing weight is harder for me than for others.

It's harder for me to choose healthy options than others.

I don't have time.

I'm too busy.

It shouldn't be this hard (success).

It shouldn't be this hard (marriage).

It shouldn't be this hard (health).

I'm doing all I can.

If I were older...

If I were younger...

If I was married...

If I wasn't married...

If I had kids...

If I didn't have kids...

If I had more money...

Money is the root of all evil.

Exercise:

Write down 5 erroneous beliefs you currently hold

1. _____

2. _____

3. _____

4. _____

5. _____

## Limiting Beliefs

You cannot both defend your limiting beliefs and overcome them. Limiting beliefs are belief systems which keep us from progressing or accomplishing what we could accomplish with a better underlying belief system.

Limiting beliefs can be erroneous beliefs, but many times, they are simply incomplete belief systems or belief systems suffering from missing perspectives.

As an example, in the late 1800s, it was a common belief people could not fly. It was clearly against the laws of physics and gravity. While this belief is true, and still human beings can't fly unassisted, we can fly to anywhere on the globe in a matter of hours through our harnessing of the laws of physics and mechanical power. "People can't fly" is a limiting belief. People can fly and have the experience of flight through the creation of the airplane. You might not have the

> **YOU CANNOT BOTH DEFEND YOUR LIMITING BELIEFS AND OVERCOME THEM.**

skills or connections to accomplish your dream right now. That may be true, but it doesn't mean you can't acquire the skills and resources needed to accomplish it. The limiting belief causes us to not look for solutions outside our current limits. The opportunity belief system says, "There are solutions; I just need to find them."

**Examples of limiting beliefs:**

**I'm not smart enough.**
**I don't have the right connections.**
**It's probably not going to work out.**
**I've tried this before and it hasn't worked out.**
**I'm not cut out for this.**
**I'm not good at sales.**
**I'm not attractive enough.**
**I'm not tech savvy enough.**
**I might do the work and still not win.**
**I know someone who tried and failed.**
**What will they think about me?**
**What if I fail?**

## WRITE DOWN 5 LIMITING BELIEFS HOLDING YOU BACK

1. _____

2. _____

3. _____

4. _____

5. _____


**Empowering Beliefs**

We are our only limit.

An empowering belief is one which creates expectant action in the direction of a goal or dream. Empowering beliefs lead to action; limiting beliefs lead to inaction. An empowering belief will always be grounded in truth and is solution oriented. While a limiting belief about money may be "I never have enough money," an empowering belief would be, "When I learn more about how to make money, I

> **LIFE ISN'T GOING TO GIVE YOU WHAT YOU WANT OR WHAT YOU WOULD LOVE TO HAVE. IN THE END, IT'S GOING TO GIVE YOU WHAT YOU ACCEPT.**

will have more money." They both acknowledge a current circumstance, but the empowering belief holds within it the seed of the solution. Another example of an empowering belief might be, "I'm not very good at this yet, but if I study those who are better than me, I will improve."

Empowering beliefs hold the accelerant to action because they provide direction and motivation to act.

**Examples of empowering beliefs:**

**Anything is learnable.**
**Given enough time, I can learn anything.**
**My current situation is not permanent.**

I am capable of becoming more.

I will do more than I'm paid for.

My raise becomes effective when I do.

Every loss has a lesson.

Other's opinions can't stop me; only I can stop me.

## Standards

A standard is a belief about how your life will be and what you will accept from it. I've never heard a great person thank "the minimums" for their success.

Don't be a minimums sort of player, doing only the minimum to get by. No one GREAT ever credited their accomplishments to "doing the minimums." Standards—what we expect and will accept out of life—are a permeating, underlying belief system which ultimately filters all our actions. Life isn't going to give you what you want or what you would love to have. In the end, it's going to give you what you accept.

Our standards set our equilibrium. We all have standards for our income, our health, what we eat, or the people we would consider as a potential spouse. These standards

> IT'S NOT THAT WHAT YOU WANT IS TOO HARD,
> IT'S THAT WHAT YOU SETTLE FOR COMES TOO EASY.

are affecting our actions twenty-four hours a day.

The question is, are your standards by design or by default? It's not that what you want is too hard, it's that what you settle for comes too easy. Raise your standards. Expect more from yourself and others. Get around others who can be standard bearers in your life, who force you to level up and stay up.

## THE NATURAL STATE

Growth is the natural state. Look at a tree for example. Have you ever seen it reading a self-help book about how to bloom more effectively? Have you ever seen a motivational speaker pumping it up saying, "Tree, I believe in you"? Yet it grows, reproduces, and multiplies. Growth is the natural state of existence. If you aren't growing, you are dying. This statement is true in nature and our lives. Since every piece of the TBAR process is simultaneously the byproduct of the piece before and the input for the next piece in the sequence, it is important to carefully examine and understand each piece in the process for optimal results.

If the right results are the byproduct of right action, and right action the byproduct of right believing, right believing is then the byproduct of right thinking. Right thinking, given time, ultimately produces the right results. Wrong or

> **GROWTH IS THE NATURAL STATE OF EXISTENCE.**
> **IF YOU AREN'T GROWING, YOU ARE DYING.**

misaligned thinking produces results not in alignment with our desired outcomes. One of the most important questions to ask yourself is, "Are my thoughts serving me?" If you are consistently dealing with non-optimal outcomes in your life, the answer is NO. There are thoughts you hold that are now holding you.

# 12

# WHEN THE STARS ALIGN

I n my experience, the belief section of TBAR is the cause of the greatest frustration, and simultaneously, once understood, the catalyst for the biggest breakthroughs on your success journey. The reason for this is that it is at the level of belief where the TBAR process automates. Here, it moves out of the conscious realm of reason and into the subconscious realm of autonomous operation. Sometimes very small tweaks in your belief system is all it takes for massive results. Conversely, many undesirable outcomes originate from false or limiting beliefs and are never detected because they are operating autonomously behind the scenes of our conscious thought. They disguise themselves as part of who we are.

I recently took part in the escape room phenomenon with my family and several friends. In an escape room, you are locked in a themed room with the other players with one goal—to get out of the room before the timer runs out. In order to get out of the room, you must locate, understand, and use clues relating to the theme to follow a process of escape. Some clues are readily visible while others are locked inside lockboxes which must be opened with the information gathered from previous clues. One of the most frustrating parts of the experience happens when you have uncovered all the clues and have all the numbers on a lock correct and in the correct order, but if even one of them is just a millimeter out of line, the lock won't open. This begins causing you to doubt whether or not you were working on the right lock or if the code or combination was even correct.

> **THE TRUTH IS, RIGHT NOW, YOU ARE PROBABLY A LOT CLOSER THAN YOU THINK TO A MAJOR BREAKTHROUGH.**

Eventually, I caught on to the importance of having the code exactly lined up. If they weren't in perfect alignment, the lock wouldn't open. Once they were aligned exactly, boom! It popped right open.

This is kind of how our lives are. We can have the right combination, the right inputs, the right actions, but if our beliefs are not in exact alignment, our code doesn't work. The truth is, right now, you are probably a lot closer than you think to a major breakthrough. You have the pieces you need; they are in the right order, they just need to be aligned.

## THE POWER OF ALIGNMENT

When our beliefs are not in alignment with our goals, our action will always be inconsistent and lacking the emotional commitment necessary to do it big. Going back to the DiSC assessment referenced earlier in the book, we all have two styles: our natural style and our adapted style.

Our natural style is who we are. It is our thoughts and beliefs as they are, not as we wish them to be. It is our true self. It is the operating system we have naturally created through the existing TBAR byproduct process.

Our adapted style is our conscious self. The self we believe we need to be, the thoughts, beliefs, and skills we think or believe or wish we would possess. It is the us we believe is necessary to accomplish our goals.

In a study of the DiSC profile we used amongst our top producers, we uncovered an incredible correlation. The people who were consistently at the top of their game, had the best attitudes, and were overall the most stable, both in business and at home, had very little degree of separation on their DiSC scatter plots between their natural and adapted self. In other words, there was an alignment between who they actually are and the person they believe they need to be. Their byproduct process was functioning and delivering to them the results they wanted quite naturally. The people whose natural and adapted styles were more divergent tended to have more inconsistency in their performance and tended to be more inconsistent overall. Misalignment in the belief section of the TBAR process acts as a roadblock to the process in general. Like a faucet turned off, it blocks the natural flow of the belief into action.

## THE POWER OF DESTINY

The idea of a calling or destiny is, in large part, a self-fulfilling prophecy. When we really believe we are supposed to do or be something great, we are able to take consistent, long range actions in that direction. Viktor Frankl, in his book *Man's Search for Meaning*, said this: "When we know why, we can endure almost any how." We are not easily deterred by negative feedback and press on towards our calling when we believe we have one. Belief around these two areas has more to do with the overall direction of someone's life than almost anything else. The

> DON'T HOLD SO TIGHTLY TO YOUR IDEA OF HOW IT'S SUPPOSED TO HAPPEN YOU MISS WHAT GOD IS TRYING TO GIVE YOU.

idea that there is something we are meant to do, or be a part of, is a powerful byproduct inducer. It can give us the extra strength, resolve, and relentlessness required to push past where others stop. There is a difference, however, between calling and destiny.

People believe a calling tends to be very specific. They might believe they are called to a specific church, vocation, or company. While that can be helpful, as we will explore in a moment, it can also be harmful to the byproduct process. Remember, the byproduct process is CREATIVE. Our beliefs create activity. Sometimes that activity produces results in line with our goals and desires but by routes different than we would have chosen consciously.

The idea of a "calling" is largely about something we feel or believe we are supposed to do or be a part of. We think we are called to be a part of this church, or to this sort of profession, or to attend this school. We believe God Has ordained something in our lives to be a certain way.

On the other hand, the idea of destiny is that you will be a part of something great or will be great yourself but is not necessarily tied to a how. The idea of destiny tends to be much more loosely focused on the "what's" and "how's," and more open, overall, on how the outcome will unfold. While the idea of destiny, in large part, becomes a self-fulfilling prophecy, the idea of calling frequently hinders people from the very destiny they believe they are pursuing. In a sermon, pastor and best-selling author Steven Furtick said this about calling: "You are called to glorify God in whatever you are doing. Outside of that, find another word for everything else. You are not called to a profession or a position at a church, you are called to bring Glory to God."

> **THERE HAS NEVER BEEN BEFORE, AND THERE WILL NEVER BE AGAIN, ANOTHER YOU.**

Many well-intentioned people are holding so tightly to their idea of how their destiny will be brought about, they miss incredible opportunities presenting themselves. Don't hold so tightly to your idea of how it's supposed to happen you miss what God is trying to give you. We need to be careful to not be so sure of what we think we want that we won't take something better.

While this isn't a spiritual book per se, and definitely isn't designed to tell you what to believe, I would be in error to not share my belief and the reasoning behind it for the purpose of illustrating the destiny concept.

There is only one of you on the entire planet, one person with your fingerprint, your specific genetic makeup, your strengths, and your weaknesses. There has never been before, and there will never be again, another you. You are uniquely qualified, with your skills, passions, and heart, to leave your mark on the world. The odds of you being here right now reading this book are so slim, it's almost mathematically incalculable. For at least 6,000 years of recorded human history, two individual people had to meet, have children, keep those children alive long enough to get to the age where their children could have children. Those children had to be in the right city, at the right time, in the right country over and over and over again, hundreds of times. When you look back, literally thousands of unique people had to be in the right place at the right time, meeting the right people across countries and even continents for countless generations for you to be here today. Everybody at the right place at the right time, every time, since the beginning of time, just for you to be here right now. This same phenomenon happened with your spouse, and it will continue with your children. You are here for a reason. You are reading this book for a reason. You were designed before the beginnings of the earth for this place and this time, and you are destined to leave your mark on this generation. If you weren't, you wouldn't be here. You, and only you, have a gift, a future, and a destiny that is totally unique to you.

This is MY belief. Whether you agree or not right now is not important. Let's look however, at the TBAR byproduct created by this belief.

If you believe you were created on purpose for a purpose, the natural byproduct is to take action to discover and fulfill that purpose. The belief there is something uniquely yours to accomplish gives you a sense of responsibility to discover and act on that uniqueness. It beckons you to revolt against the status quo. You look for opportunities to create impact. You search out and pursue greatness. Why? You believe it's what you are supposed to do. What result does this mindset and its corresponding byproduct produce? World changers and people who leave their mark.

Now, let's take a look at the opposite of this belief. You believe you are not here for any specific reason. You are just basically primordial ooze that crawled out of the swamp a few million years ago and evolved into a random human being.

> **YOU, AND ONLY YOU, HAVE A GIFT, A FUTURE, AND A DESTINY THAT IS TOTALLY UNIQUE TO YOU.**

Random chance happens over and over again with no purpose and no plan, and bang! Here you are. You will live, and die, and none of it really matters. it's all just a cosmic accident.

Any wonder depression rates are so high?

If this is your belief, then what you do doesn't really matter. Why? Well, because you don't really matter. Such a belief creates actions and inactions consistent with itself.

I view the belief pattern around destiny as fundamental and core. In other words, what you believe here affects almost every other belief pattern you have. If you don't know what you believe in this area, I would encourage you to research, to ask the tough questions, and to FOLLOW TRUTH. If you want more resources or to talk with someone about your questions in this area, please contact us through the email address listed in the resource section of this book.

## HOLD TIGHTLY TO THE WHY AND LOOSELY TO THE HOW

American inventor and businessman Thomas Edison, often described as America's greatest inventor, credited with the building and development of many devices, said: "So many people miss their opportunity because it is dressed in overalls and looks like work."

Let me give you an example from my own experience. I have always believed my life would be important, and I would be part of something great. Earning $27,000 a year with no influence and the weight of the world starting to drag on me, this vision wasn't looking like reality. Yet, I still believed. My belief created action. I wrote a book (not this one), recorded a demo CD (I know. This shows my age), and started in business. I was not tied to HOW my life would change, just that it would, indeed, change. Honestly in a million years, I wouldn't have picked the method

> SO MANY PEOPLE MISS THEIR OPPORTUNITY BECAUSE IT IS DRESSED IN OVERALLS AND LOOKS LIKE WORK.

God used to bless my life. Out of countless tries, I wouldn't have guessed it. Here's the key—I was open to the possibilities of destiny. I wasn't tied to a calling; having to accomplish it in a certain way. People who feel heavily that they are called to do a certain thing often miss what God is trying to do in their lives because it doesn't look like they thought it would. After all, God is the one who sent a baby in a manger when what they were expecting was a king on the throne.

## God Sees Our Plans and Laughs

In my own personal life, something I wasn't expecting came across my path. It was an opportunity I had never thought of before and really had no initial affinity towards. I was working in a field at the time I really enjoyed. Many would have said I was "called" to do this certain thing. In fact, many did. I always had a high degree of belief in destiny but a relatively low level of belief in the concept of calling. Because of this, I was able to be open minded enough to recognize the movement of God in my life, bringing me something I wasn't expecting but would, in hindsight, revolutionize my entire life. God brings us opportunities, people, and influence many times in unexpected ways. Unfortunately, most people are

> **GOD BRINGS US OPPORTUNITIES, PEOPLE, AND INFLUENCE MANY TIMES IN UNEXPECTED WAYS.**

unwilling to recognize it and take advantage of the opportunity because it doesn't look like they thought it would. Don't get so caught up with what you have and where you are that you can't recognize the next level when it comes. Be excellent where you are, with what you have. Prepare, grow, and develop, and stay open to opportunities that find you. The fact is, the belief systems that got you where you are today are not going to take you to the next level tomorrow.

## Beliefs ALWAYS Create Action

"Preach... all the time, and if necessary use words," is one of my favorite phrases. The world is full of people who want to share their opinions, when what we need is people who will share their example. Let our lives be the testimony of the things we believe in. As the TBAR process transforms our beliefs into action, our lives inevitably become the screen on which our beliefs play out for the world to see.

# SECTION FIVE
## ACTIONS

# 13

# THE FOUR STAGES OF COMPETENCE

## SUCCESS DOESN'T COME FROM WHAT YOU DO OCCASIONALLY; IT COMES FROM WHAT YOU DO CONSISTENTLY.

A nything worth doing is worth overdoing. MASSIVE action in the direction of your dreams is the most direct connection to the life and significance you desire. Action has, and always will be, the most direct causation of the results you have now. If you want to change your results, you must change something you are doing on a daily basis. As we begin to harness and direct our

**ANYTHING WORTH DOING IS WORTH OVERDOING.**

actions, it's important to understand the four levels at which action occurs. Let's explore the psychological concept of the four stages of competence.

**Four stages:**

Unconscious Incompetence
Conscious Incompetence
Conscious Competence
Unconscious Competence

## FOUR STAGES OF COMPETENCE

| UNCONSCIOUS INCOMPETENCE | UNCONSCIOUS COMPETENCE |
|---|---|
| You are unaware of the skill and your lack of proficiency | Performing the skill becomes automatic |
| CONSCIOUS INCOMPETENCE | CONSCIOUS COMPETENCE |
| You are aware of the skill but not yet proficient | You are able to use the skill, but only with effort |

## NOT ALL ACTION IS CREATED EQUAL

### Unconscious Incompetence

At this stage, we are so novice with the action we are taking, we simply don't know what we don't know. We are playing soccer on a basketball court, running up and down the field flailing about, tiring ourselves out, with no chance to score. This is unexamined action, or action taken without direction. It's busyness. Action for the purpose of action instead of action for the purpose of outcome. At this level, we are unaware that what we are doing isn't working, won't work, and that change is required. Think William Hung on *American Idol*. Bless his heart. He's bad, but he doesn't know he's bad, so he just keeps on singing.

### Conscious Incompetence

At this stage, we realize what we are doing isn't working. We are aware we aren't very good. This is the salesman who can't close and knows something needs to change. Our awareness allows us to ask questions about our action, and to seek out better and more accurate action.

## Conscious Competence

At this level, we are competent at our actions, but they require conscious effort to maintain competence. It requires effort and focus at every step. It's like the new driver who is just learning to drive. Every move must be analyzed and thought through. It is highly inefficient, but it works. We get results, but it takes a lot of effort. Conscious competence is where most people try to interrupt the byproduct process by injecting new actions into the sequence. They consciously choose a new action, trying to override the natural action underneath. The problem with doing this is, because the new behavior wasn't a byproduct of the underlying thinking and belief, it takes conscious effort to insert it and keep it active.

While you can force new action at the conscious level, only the action which turns into habit, an unconscious competence, will produce lasting and effortless change.

Think about the process of an action creating a result likened to a space shuttle getting ready to lift off the ground. As the space shuttle fires its thrusters to get lift off, it is one of the most inefficient processes known to man. Burning literally thousands of gallons of fuel per second to get the rocket just a few feet off the ground, the effort expended is largely unsustainable. As it continues to accelerate off the ground, the fuel burn is immense. It's so taxing, the shuttle, if required to burn fuel the entire trip at the same rate it burns it at the start, wouldn't make it more than an hour into its mission. This is similar to the action spend in our lives. The input of action is front-loaded and much larger than one would expect. By the time the space shuttle breaks the drag of the atmosphere, it has burned up nearly all of its fuel. It can, however, now orbit the earth almost effortlessly, burning little to no fuel and traveling around the planet at a rate of over 20,000 miles an hour. Success is a lot like that space shuttle—it takes massive action, an unsustainable action, really, in the beginning to just get it off the ground. There is no moderate effort or middle of the road. It is an intense, immense, and constant burn which allows your life to lift off. Without the massive front-loaded action, the space shuttle, just like many people's lives and dreams, never gets off the ground.

Breaking through the atmosphere is a lot like the stage of conscious competence. It's still taking large amounts of focused effort, although, now you have momentum assisting in the burn. It's still work, it's still effort, but you begin to see results in this stage or at least the appearance that you are moving more quickly in the direction of the outcome than you were before.

When the shuttle finally breaks the Earth's atmosphere, it gives one final thrust where, unimpeded by the drag of the atmosphere (issues and choices), it can circle the globe at unimaginable speed. This is the phase of unconscious competence or habit.

Consider this riddle that I came across:

Who am I?

I am your constant companion.

I am your greatest helper or heaviest burden.

I will push you onward or drag you down to failure.

I am completely at your command.

Half the things you do you might just as well turn over to me, and I will be able to do them quickly, correctly.

I am easily managed - you must merely be firm with me. Show me exactly how you want something done, and after a few lessons, I will do it automatically.

I am the servant of all great people; and alas, of all failures as well. Those who are failures, I have made failures.

I am not a machine, though I work with all the precision of a machine, plus the intelligence of a human being.

You may run me for a profit or turn me for ruin - it makes no difference to me.

Take me, train me, be firm with me, and I will place the world at your feet.

Be easy with me and I will destroy you.

Who am I?

I AM HABIT.

-Anonymous

## Unconscious Competence

At this level of action, our actions are merely byproducts of the thinking and belief which created them. They are natural. They occur effortlessly for the holder of the habit. When our actions have become habit, we no longer need to think about them, we just do them. They become part of who we are. They take little to no effort to complete.

NOTE: When creating a habit intentionally, it is imperative to reinforce the action by creating thought processes and beliefs which are the natural components of the action. Without the constant, never ceasing influence of the new thought and belief, the existing thoughts and beliefs will eventually recreate the previous habit. This is evident all around us as we see people start new diets every New Year. They eat better, they join a gym, and they get results... for a while. But almost inevitably, the weight comes back. Why? We forced a conscious change to our action, but we didn't reprogram the underlying beliefs causing the weight gain to begin with. Over time, the unconscious belief, through sheer power and persistence, undoes the conscious training.

We all have habits, and research shows up to 97% of the decisions and actions we make are made at the unconscious or habit level. The problem is, for many of us, our habits weren't chosen on purpose. They were chosen for us by default, as a byproduct of our unexamined thinking and belief systems.

Massive action in the direction of our goals, partnered with the inspection and installation of aligned thoughts and beliefs (thoughts and beliefs that would naturally create the forced action pattern), is the best way to jumpstart the creation of your desired outcome. Working both angles, the new action and the underlying thoughts and beliefs, speed up the process of creating new byproduct patterns. When combined, they create a self-realizing cycle—the action creates results, albeit temporary, which reinforce the new thoughts and belief patterns. The new thoughts and belief patterns reinforce the actions, and you begin the cycle of success.

# 14

# THE ACTION QUOTIENT

## AMPLITUDE X PRECISION X TIME = RESULT

W hen our thinking and believing are correct, it always leads to correct action. But "correct" may not be enough to create the results we desire by itself. There are three things necessary for the action we take to create the desired byproduct result.

### THE ACTION QUOTIENT

AMPLITUDE  X  PRECISION  X  TIME  =  RESULT

## AMPLITUDE

Many times, people are doing the right things, they just aren't doing the right things in enough volume to get the shuttle off the launch pad. Think about success like boiling water. At 212 degrees, you can run a steam ship, cook food, and sanitize virtually anything. At 211 degrees, all you have is hot water. It's only off by one degree, but it creates all the difference. Success is a critical mass ball game. You must break the activity threshold to get lift off. Often, we are doing the right thing, just simply not enough of it. The first place we should look when we are working diligently but not experiencing the results we seek is amplitude. "Am I doing enough of the correct action?" Assuming our thinking and beliefs are accurate, our action will be correct, it is the volume of action we are taking which is most likely the culprit. Virtually everyone looks to a deficiency in skill set before looking to a deficiency in activity, yet almost always, more activity is the answer. Since the right thinking and right believing always creates the right action, we are

> **DON'T BE THE PERSON WITH A FIVE-YEAR VISION AND THREE WEEK WORK ETHIC.**

probably very close to the action needed to create what we want. But that doesn't necessarily mean we are taking action the right amount. Many well-meaning people are deceived, thinking they will get big results with small actions. When it comes to taking action, there are three sorts of people in the world:

**The Thief, the Gambler, and the Champion**

One of my good friends, author and speaker Collis Temple III, shared a concept with me that essentially all people, when it comes to taking action, are one of these three sorts of people.

**The Thief**

The thief wants something for nothing. Instead of putting in effort to earn something, they would rather steal what someone else has earned. They want a free lunch. Just the fact you have purchased this book and have read this far, you have basically guaranteed this is not you!

**The Gambler**

The gambler is someone who puts in a little bit but expects a massive return. They put in a little money, but they expect big money in return. They put in a little time but expect massive results. They put in a little effort at the gym but want to look like the person training four hours a day. Their desired result and amount of action are not in alignment. Their input of action is far below the necessary threshold for the result they desire. In truth, this is most people. They desire a certain outcome, and even take action in the direction, but fall short of achieving

**EVERYONE TODAY TALKS ABOUT BEING RELENTLESS, BUT RELENTLESS IS A DIFFERENT ANIMAL.**

the goal. It may have even been the correct action, just not enough of it to create critical mass. They are 211-degree people.

### The Champion

The champion pays the price and expects to win. The champion isn't afraid of the effort. They take massive action, they overdo, they leave nothing to chance. They guarantee, through their effort, the amount of action required is completed. If the price is $20, the champion pays $30. There is no question in the champion's mind—they deserve what they have worked for.

Don't be the person with a five-year vision and three week work ethic. Be known as the hardest worker in the room. Right now, there are people less talented than you, from harder backgrounds than you, with less going for them than you, who are living the life you dream about living. The fact is this: they are outworking you. Hard work beats talent when talent doesn't work hard. There is value in the work itself; it makes you feel good about yourself. Winston Churchill once

**RELENTLESS IS ABOUT WHAT IS INSIDE OF YOU. IT'S YOUR HEART, AND IT IS COMPLETELY AND TOTALLY UNSTOPPABLE.**

said, "No one can guarantee success in war, but only deserve it." Though he was referring to war, his meaning applies to many areas of life where hard work is required. We should work in such a way that everyone around us believes our success is an inevitable matter of time. Get after it and go BIG if you want results others don't have. You must take your activity to a completely different level. You've got to become relentless.

There's always a way. There is a solution to every problem. Period. And a champion finds it. They attack relentlessly, regroup, refocus, and attack again until the problem, set back, or obstacle is destroyed. Everyone today talks about being relentless, but relentless is a different animal. It's a way of being where you accept no excuses on results. You become the fiercest competitor imaginable. You compete with no one; they compete with you. It's a level of excellence, consistency, and focus found only in the greats. You don't need to be relentless to win. You can have a great life and a great impact without it, but the byproduct of relentless is total greatness. It's about what you want, what you dream of, and what you will fight for. Relentless is the ability to rise above the things which would take others out and turn them to your advantage, to use the fire that would try to consume you as fuel. When there doesn't seem to be a way, you find one or you make one. Whether in business, family, or whatever it is you do, relentless is about what is inside of you. It's your heart, and it is completely and totally unstoppable.

## PRECISION

Precision is the quality and accuracy of the action. If you are in sales you will have scripts, presentations, and best practices that are known to have the highest conversion rates. Someone with low precision may take an ample amount of action but lacks the skill to convert their action into results. A potential bodybuilder may boost their calories but consume in those boosted calories too little additional protein. They may gain weight, but they won't build muscle even though they had boosted the calories to the needed level. They took action, it just wasn't totally accurate action.

> HOW WE DO THE LITTLE THINGS
> IS HOW WE DO EVERYTHING!

In other words, we can take the right action in the right amount but can be off in the QUALITY or accuracy of said action and still end up off course.

It's possible for a ship leaving harbor in NYC to be only one degree off in direction when they leave for England, and over the large distance traveled, to end up hundreds of miles off course. How we do the little things is how we do everything! Most people don't see it necessary to correct a one-degree difference. They ignore some minor wording differences in their scripts or make a tweak to the macros their trainer recommends, but just like the ship hundreds of miles off course, we end up off course when our actions aren't precise.

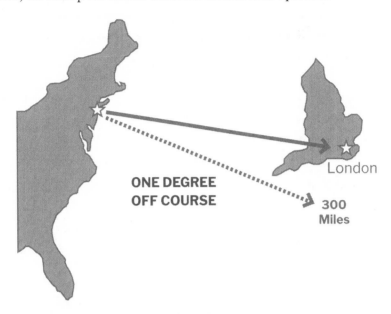

ONE DEGREE
OFF COURSE

London

300
Miles

**Upgraded Action: Skills Pay the Bills**

While it is absolutely true that the correct underlying thinking and belief systems create action in the direction of the dream, it is important to realize not all actions are created equal. For example, you may think flying an airplane would be incredible. You think you would love it. You may believe you could learn to fly with enough training and practice. This belief may lead you to take the action of enrolling in flight school, getting into a plane, and trying to learn how to fly. The problem is, you have never flown, and although you are taking action in the direction of your dream, you don't have the skill or knowledge required to create your desired outcome… yet. The byproduct of your belief may be the attempt to fly the plane. Your

> SKILLS ARE THE WEAPONS WITH WHICH YOU WAGE THE WAR OF SUCCESS.

lack of preparation and skill may lead to the crashing of the plane moments later. Skills pay the bills, and in the aforementioned example, skills may keep you alive.

Think about skills in this way—skills are the weapons with which you wage the war of success. Two hundred years ago, the ACTION of warfare was taken very differently than it is today. The weapons of warfare were very different than they are today. Two hundred years ago, warfare was fought hand to hand, musket against musket. Today, warfare can be made from drones in remote locations. A single deployment of a nuclear weapon can demolish entire cities. The ACTION of warfare happened then, and it happens now. The weapons of warfare have upgraded and can accomplish much more today with much less effort. This is what happens when we upgrade our skills. Upgraded skills make our actions more potent and accelerate the speed and scope of byproduct success. Many people go into the battle for success with skill sets and mindsets that are underdeveloped and antiquated. While they do take action in the direction of their dreams as a byproduct of correct thinking and believing, their action isn't as effective as it could be, and sometimes is not effective at all.

## TIME

All great things take time. Seed time and harvest speaks to the process farmers take from planting to yielding their crop. There is a time for planting (input) and a time for reaping (byproduct), but in between these two events is TIME. See the example below of a penny doubled every day.

### ONE CENT DOUBLED EACH DAY FOR A MONTH

| 1 $.01 | 1 $.02 | 3 $.04 | 4 $.08 | 5 $.16 | 6 $.32 | 7 $.64 |
|---|---|---|---|---|---|---|
| 8 $1.28 | 9 $2.56 | 10 $5.12 | 11 $10.24 | 12 $20.48 | 13 $40.96 | 14 $81.92 |
| 15 $163.48 | 16 $327.68 | 17 $655.36 | 18 $1,310.72 | 19 $2,621.44 | 20 $5,242.88 | 21 $10,485.76 |
| 22 $20,971.52 | 23 $41,943.04 | 24 $83,886.08 | 25 $167,772.16 | 26 $335,544.32 | 27 $671,088.64 | 28 $1,342,177.28 |
| 29 $2,684,354.56 | 30 $5,368,709.12 | 31 $10,737,418.24 | | | | |

In this example, the unit of time is a day, but you could make the time unit a week, a month, or a year, and the compounding function would work exactly the same. Compounding interest, like compounding efforts, is a function of time. As the last part of the equation, it is the final factor in turning action into results. You must take enough (amplitude) of the correct (precision) action consistently over a long enough period of time to allow for the effort to compound. You can be on the right track, but if you just stand there, you are going to get run over. People start a business but give it six months when a business can take three to five years to become profitable. People eat right and exercise for thirty days, but when they don't see the results, they give up. You must allow for the full, appropriate passage of time; doing the right things in the right amount to lead to your right byproduct.

A note to the reader here about time. The time factor must be applied in a consecutive fashion. In other words, it must be an uninterrupted passage of time applied to the action. For example, if you take the penny out for five days, you won't end up anywhere near the number you had before. Even though the five days still passed, they didn't pass in the compounding process. The time passed but wasn't applied to the activity of the penny doubling. When you pull your penny out of the market, the clock stops.

Many people try to create new habits but only act on it on weekdays. The problem with this approach is studies show it takes approximately sixty-three days to create a new habit. The designer of the habit only gets five days in before the sixty-three day process is interrupted. Every Monday, they start over again but at day one, not at day six. Approaching it this way, the habit never forms. One of my mentors, Hector Lamarque, known across the financial industry for building an agency of 10,000 + licensed agents, said for every day in the beginning you waste not focused on outcome producing activity, you add four days to the time it will take you to achieve your goal. The power of consistency is everything.

## Implementation

So, how do we effectively learn and implement the action quotient? There's are a few things you can do and a few processes you can implement to evaluate your effectiveness in the action quotient. All of them involve having a trusted mentor with the results you desire.

1. Get a mentor. Learning from our mistakes is experience, learning from the mistakes of others is wisdom. Find a mentor who has had the success and the outcome you

**LISTEN, DON'T TALK; YOU ARE THERE TO LEARN FROM YOUR MENTOR, NOT FOR YOUR MENTOR TO LEARN FROM YOU.**

desire and learn from them. In the beginning, like it was for me, it may only be possible to be mentored from afar through the books, podcasts, and YouTube videos your chosen mentor has produced. If you are fortunate enough to have the attention of your mentor, get all you can from it. Listen, don't talk; you are there to learn from your mentor, not for your mentor to learn from you.

2. Don't be an ask-hole. That's someone who takes the mentor's time, solicits advice, but then doesn't take it or doesn't act on it. They always want to know more but never act on the information. Act on what your mentor tells you.

3. Ask the mentor for bold and truthful feedback, and be resolved to take everything the mentor says, no matter how hard it is to hear. It is especially important to seek feedback about how you are performing on the action quotient. Ask questions such as: Do you believe I'm taking enough action to achieve my desired goal? Do you believe I am missing any skills or abilities necessary to achieve my goals? Do you believe I am performing consistently enough to realize my desired outcome? How do you feel about my progress based on the amount of time I have been pursuing this outcome? Is there anything I don't see which I must change in order to win?

# 15

## ACTION FOR THE LONG HAUL

In the action quotient, the function of time and staying consistent over longer periods of time than you might expect can prove to be one of the most challenging facets of winning big. The journey towards your goals and dreams often starts with pure excitement. When the finish line is in sight, the sheer adrenaline of attaining that for which you have fought can be enough to pull you across the goal line. It's in the middle, when the work becomes tedious and tiresome, where the finish line is not yet in sight, that most people abandon ship. One of the greatest tools you can use to stay motivated in the middle is the mastery and harnessing of your own motivation combination.

### The Motivation Combination

In his book *Awaken the Giant,* leadership expert Tony Robbins asserts people are primarily motivated by two things:

1. The pursuit of pleasure

2. The avoidance of pain

While everyone will experience both types of motivation, it is typical for individuals to be dominant in one of the two motivators. Discussed briefly in earlier chapters, we will take a deep dive into understanding our motivation combination here.

I like to call people who are generally more responsive to the pursuit of pleasure "carrot people." Like a donkey being directed by the dangling carrot in front of them, they move in whatever direction the carrot moves. These people are motivated by the prospect of gain, winning contests, and the thrill of victory.

I call people who are generally more responsive to the avoidance of pain "stick people." The carrot does little for them, and they tend only to disrupt their current path to avoid pain. Like the donkey prodded to move with a whack of the stick, these people respond to impending pain. They will do little to make changes until pain is a reality.

Again, while we may react in both ways circumstantially, we tend to operate primarily from one of the two operating systems. As we discuss the levels of motivation, it will be useful for us to view them through the perspective of carrot person or stick person.

In their book *Launching a Leadership Revolution*, Chris Brady and Orrin Woodward talk about the three levels of motivation. They make a statement that "hunger is a discipline," and one of the primary roles of a leader is to make sure their hunger and motivation stays intact and growing. We briefly touched on the three levels of motivation earlier, but here, we will explore them in more depth. There are three basic levels of motivation operating internally in people, each with an ascending level of drive and intensity. As we go through each of the three levels, I will give you a couple practical exercises you can implement to increase your level of motivation.

## FIRST LEVEL – MATERIAL MOTIVATION

We are all materially motivated first for our own well-being by things like food and shelter, then our general well-being, followed by a desire and affinity for the finer things in life. Sometimes I hear people say in a false piousness they are not motivated by material things. This is false. If you were to lose your job and your home or car, or your ability to feed your family was in jeopardy, you would take actions necessary to keep these things from happening. That is material motivation. Everyone is motivated materially. The problem is most people's material motivation has been deactivated. In other words, their material needs and desires have lowered to fit their incomes. Instead of raising their incomes to achieve the desired level of material motivation, they lower the motivation. Make no mistake, you can, through practice and purposeful retraining, raise your level of motivation to any level you choose. This proves extremely helpful when trying to keep yourself moving towards your long-range goal. The problem with material motivation is it is the shallowest level of motivation, not wrong or subpar, but rather, once the material desire is acquired, it ceases to motivate you.

### Material Motivation for Carrot People

1. Set intermediate targets and input goals and tie them to rewards. Instead of just buying things you want, create a reward system for yourself. Even though you may have the capacity to purchase what you desire,

> **MOST PEOPLE WOULD RATHER LOOK RICH THAN GET RICH.**

delay it until the achievement of your goal. Most people would rather LOOK rich than get rich. Don't buy it because you can, buy it because you earned it. Delayed gratification is a powerful use of material motivation for the carrot person. Continue to set escalating rewards in turn for achieving escalated goals.

2. Upgrade your life. When you buy your next airline ticket, upgrade your seat by one level. On your next rental car, upgrade it one level. When you buy your next concert ticket, get one level better seats than you are accustomed to sitting in now. These small upgrades will give you an awareness that higher levels exist and what they are like. They are small costs but create experiences which stay with you and cause you to think differently about your material motivations. You begin to raise the level of your equilibrium. Just be careful not to supersize your life too fast.

3. Test drive your future. One of the things I did a lot during the early years of my business was to test drive the cars I eventually wanted to own. I would pull

into the dealership, sit in the car and take in all the senses of the experience, the feel, the smell, the sight. I would inquire into the payments and figure out what I needed to earn to be able to get it. I would do the same things with model homes in beautiful neighborhoods. I would walk through models every chance I got because it gave me a vision about what life could be like. Maybe your goal is permanent

> ONCE THE HUMAN MIND IS EXPANDED, IT CAN NEVER SHRINK BACK TO ITS ORIGINAL STATE.

weight loss, then buy a dress you love in the size you want to be. Put it in a prominent place where you can see it every day. Give yourself a concrete vision of what you are working towards. Once the human mind is expanded, it can never shrink back to its original state. Stoke your flame with material motivation.

**Material Motivation for Stick People**

1.  Since stick people generally don't move until there is sufficient pain, the name of the game becomes creating an artificial pain before the onset of actual pain. If you are in sales, you will begin to take massive action a week before the mortgage payment is due to avoid a delinquent payment. Instead of living a reactionary life on the edge of real disaster, champions learn to set up artificial pain points.

Earlier in my career, one of my mentors suggested we set up a $1500 per month auto-draft into an investment account for the 15th of every month. If you are too comfortable where you are, set up an auto-draft, and one of two things will happen—you will chicken out and stop it or you will work to have the income to meet the withdrawal. What was he doing? He was creating an artificial pain with the withdrawal which mimicked the pain of an impending bill. This creates a demand for action, forcing you to not only take action but to move your finances forward.

He told me every time I felt financially comfortable, simply increase the auto draft, and poof! Magically, you are broke again. Comfort is the enemy of success. Get comfortable being uncomfortable!

2. Material accountability is another great tool for stick people at the first level of motivation. Put your money where your mouth is. Tell your goal to a trusted friend, accountability group, or mentor and create a system where by, when you do not make your goal, you pay a small fine. For the stick person, the avoidance of even a small fine will often do more to motivate them than the acquisition of a goal many times the size of the fine.

The key here is it doesn't really matter if you are a carrot or a stick person, as long as you know which you are and are willing to take the steps to harness every level of motivation.

## SECOND LEVEL – RESPECT AND RECOGNITION

All humans have an intrinsic need for respect and crave recognition deeply. Harnessing the power of respect and recognition can be an extremely powerful tool to finish the job. I hear people say all the time some version of, "If you want to be successful, you can't care about what others think." This is total trash. We all care about what others think, the problem is most of us care about what the wrong people think. We should worry about pleasing our mentors and coaches instead of the guy in the cubicle next to us.

Often, we care more about what our detractors and discouragers think than what

> **WE ALL CARE ABOUT WHAT OTHERS THINK, THE PROBLEM IS MOST OF US CARE ABOUT WHAT THE WRONG PEOPLE THINK.**

our peers and mentors think about us. The craving to be respected by those you respect is one of the most powerful motivating forces on earth. It is a much longer lasting form of motivation than its material predecessor.

Early in my business career, I was an up and coming star within our company. One of the founders of the company, worth several hundred million dollars, had an after party at his home in the Dallas suburbs after a large training event. I was thrilled to be invited and even more thrilled when he began to give out different awards. I sat in this beautiful stone outdoor pavilion at his home and daydreamed of him calling my name. It was deeply motivating to me. Much to my surprise, I was awakened from this daydream trance by the sound of my name coming from this legend's voice. I stood up and went to the front to meet him. He handed me an award and stopped. He put his hand on my shoulder and said in front of the crowd of 300 leaders gathered at his home, "Look at you, making all this money, what an incredible job you are doing. But I've seen a thousand of you before. You probably won't be here this time next year," and sent me back to my seat. I was furious and embarrassed. I wanted nothing more than to make him know my name and to prove him wrong. And I did.

Today, he and I are incredibly close, and he has been one of the most influential mentors in my life. I wanted his respect and was willing to work for years to earn it. And then to keep it. It can take years of effort in a field to rise to the top and get yourself on the radars of the current players in that space. Getting their respect is part of the challenge,

> **THE CRAVING TO BE RESPECTED BY THOSE YOU RESPECT IS ONE OF THE MOST POWERFUL MOTIVATING FORCES ON EARTH.**

maintaining it is the next. Anyone can get to the top, but it takes character, integrity, and work ethic to stay there. Once you achieve recognition and respect from those you respect, you are highly motivated to keep it. Don't be one of those one hit wonders.

### Respect and Recognition for Carrot People

We all have people we look up to as leaders, mentors, and even heroes. One of the best tools that a carrot person can use at the second level of motivation is the drive to be able to connect with and build a meaningful relationship with those they admire. On my vision board, I have several people that I admire greatly and have the goal of establishing a relationship with them. Make a list of people you want to meet, get to know, and have as mentors in your life, and then work to get on their radar. Today, many of the people I saw as heroes and legends early on in my career, have now become personal friends. Here's the key: Earn their respect, don't seek after it. When you crush it in your field, the other players in the game take notice. Work until you no longer have to introduce yourself.

**Respect and Recognition for Stick People**

As a stick person, your primary motivator is the avoidance of pain. If you allow yourself to fly below the radar of those you admire, you will never get the leverage that respect and recognition have to offer you. Put yourself out there publicly. Proclaim your goals and intentions loud and proud to the world. The pain created by the fear of failing publicly and insight of those you respect can become an incredibly powerful motivator for sustained action.

## THIRD LEVEL – LEGACY

Your life has an expiration date; your legacy does not. In a world where most people are living for the weekend, true champions are living for the shadow which extends beyond their lifetimes. What is your life and example going to mean to the generations who come after you? Most people two or three generations removed may as well have never existed, their names and legacies forgotten through the sands of time. Think about how many generations of grandparents you can name. For

> **YOUR LIFE HAS AN EXPIRATION DATE; YOUR LEGACY DOES NOT.**

most, we can only recall a few. Four and five generations removed, we know very little, if anything at all, about them, even having spent an entire lifetime on earth.

We should seek to live in such a way where our names and our causes live for a thousand years. I want to be remembered. We all do. That's why a keen sense of legacy and destiny are such powerful motivators. Long after the feelings leave, and they all do eventually, our legacy is there calling us to greater heights and bigger vision. After all the niceties of life have been had, and everyone respects you at the top of your field, who you were and what you stood for will keep you moving.

**Legacy for Carrot People**

The concept of legacy is abstract and can't be fully understood on this side of eternity, but one of the greatest tools to leverage motivation here is to visualize what you hope your legacy will be. Get a vision of the things for which you wish to be remembered. Maybe it's a name to be revered for generations, a cure, or an invention that changed the world. What is it going to mean to you and others if you lived the best life you were capable of living? Take a few minutes and write this out. Return to it weekly to review and add to it.

**Legacy for Stick People**

Imagine, two to three generations from now, you might as well have never existed. Your life's work forgotten; your relationships forgotten. It's a sobering thought and, unfortunately, will be reality for almost everyone on the planet who doesn't set their sights on living big and making a huge impact. It is a scary truth, don't let it be yours.

# 16

## TIME KEEPS TICKING

**W**henever we decide to take massive action in the direction of our dreams, we must discuss time, priorities, and systems. We cannot add something into our life without something being subtracted.

Time is the great equalizer. We all have 168 hours a week; what we do with our time is what creates the separation between the great and the ordinary. In the next pages, you will learn several tried and tested techniques to use your time more effectively and efficiently to maximize your results.

### The Three Uses of Time

Before we discuss the how, we must first get a clear understanding of the why. When it comes to time, there are ultimately three ways in which time is used. Let's explore those now.

1.  Waste: It's better to be at the bottom of the staircase you want to climb than the top of the one you don't.

Succeeding at things that don't matter is the pastime of the average and ordinary. The first place time can go is to waste. Think about when you waste money, what has happened? We have spent money but did not get anything in return for it. The money is gone but we have nothing to show for it. This is a waste of money. Similarly, when we waste time, we put time into something or someone, but we have nothing to show for our time trade. Some common examples of wasted time are

> **SUCCEEDING AT THINGS THAT DON'T MATTER IS THE PASTIME OF THE AVERAGE AND ORDINARY.**

time spent watching TV, playing video games, or obsessing about the stats of professional sports players or teams. We can put almost endless amounts of time into these things but have nothing tangible to show for these in return. Most great successes have gotten ahead using the time other people waste.

2. Spend: The second ultimate use of time is to spend it. When you spend time, time is traded for something tangible in return. Think about when you spend money at the grocery store, the money is gone, but you have food in return. When you spend money on a car, the money is gone, but you have a car in return. In the same way, time can be spent or traded for something else of value.

What are some examples of trading time? Working is one of the most obvious time-spends. When we work, we trade large amounts of time, and in return, we receive monies needed to run our lives. Time with family is also a time-spend. You are trading time in return for rewarding relationships and fulfillment. The time is gone, but we have received something in return. For most people, time-spend represents the largest portion of their available time. Remember, time-spend is, at some level, inevitable. There will always be certain necessary time-spends for things like family, friends, and spiritual life.

3. Investment: When we invest money, we put capital in with the expectation of getting more out. An investment creates more of itself. When we invest time, we are putting time into something which yields more time than was invested. An example of a time investment would be time put into health and wellness. The time invested here will add years, or even decades, to your life. Time invested is, in turn, yielding more time.

Another investment of time is energy put into creating residual income. Once residual income in excess of our expenses is created, we no longer need to spend forty to sixty hours a week trying to earn money. We put time into the development of a business, but it yields more time than was invested. Normal thinking brings normal results. Our goal as we invest into time investment activities is to break out of the normal box which keeps people in perpetual time-spend mode.

Remember this, you can get $60k a year and a life sentence at a normal job almost anywhere. The byproduct is about building a DREAM and a LIFE; not just making a living. When you put time into building a recurring income, it costs you a season, but the freedom is forever. At the job, it costs you forever for a season of freedom. It is almost always a sacrifice and an inconvenience to invest time. But, when we miss the part of our lives called sacrifice, we miss the part of our lives called significance. Be wise! Invest in your future, one day you will have to live in it.

## WEALTH FROM WASTE

The ideal time allocation or use of time is to shift all the time from *waste* activities into *investment* activities. You can make this shift while initially maintaining the current time-spend activities. Eventually, the investment of time which used to be wasted will create better health, both physically and financially. The time invested will provide the ability to spend less time on your job, reallocating this time to other, more enjoyable spends and time investment opportunities. This is how you create total freedom in your life. It is, however, the exact opposite of

> WHEN WE MISS THE PART OF OUR LIVES CALLED SACRIFICE, WE MISS THE PART OF OUR LIVES CALLED SIGNIFICANCE.

what the average person does with their time. Average Joe leaves no time for investment, just like he leaves no money for investment and lives forever hand to mouth. It's the same with time; the average person claims to be busy like it's a status symbol, yet they are busy with time waste and spend, becoming trapped in a never-ending circle of not enough time.

Write down three things you allocate your time into in each category:

**Waste**

1. _____

2. _____

3. _____

**Spend**

1. _____

2. _____

3. _____

**Invest**

1. _____

2. _____

3. _____

What can you cut out of the first category to allocate more time towards invest and spend activities?

_____

_____

_____

# 17

# GET YOUR PRIORITIES STRAIGHT

## INSTEAD OF SAYING, "I DON'T HAVE TIME FOR THAT," NEXT TIME TRY SAYING, "IT ISN'T A PRIORITY."

Y ou can have ANYTHING you want, but you can't have everything you want, at least at the same time. Prioritization is the key to productive lives. Later made famous by Steven Covey, the Eisenhower Matrix is a massively effective tool for creating priorities and helping us to identify and eliminate time wastes. There are four types of activities monopolizing our time. Let's discuss the quadrants.

### THE EISENHOWER MATRIX

| 1<br>Urgent /<br>Important | 3<br>Not Urgent /<br>Important |
|---|---|
| 2<br>Urgent /<br>Not Important | 4<br>Not Urgent /<br>Not Important |

### Quadrant One: Urgent and Important

These are things which have a major impact on the most important areas of your life. They are also things with immediate deadlines. They are things that can only be done by you. If they don't meet all three criteria, they are not important and urgent. This might be a deadline at work, a dinner with your spouse for their birthday, or your little guy's little league World Series game. In these instances, NO ONE CAN REPLACE YOU, and they can't be done any other time. These are generally demands on our time from outside our direct control. These must be done by us, and they (the demands) let us know.

### Quadrant Two: Urgent Not Important

These are also things requiring immediate attention but are not material to the outcome of your life. This could be a flat tire on the way to work, doing the laundry or dishes, mowing the lawn, grocery shopping, etc. They are things needing attention but are not necessarily required to be done by you.

### Quadrant Three: Important Not Urgent

These things are critical to the outcome of your goals and dreams. They are material to your life's aim. They must be done by you, but there are no pending deadlines. These are things like exercise, self-development, creating recurring income, and reading. All of these things help us to be the best, most productive version of ourselves. They are the tools with which we will erect the skyscraper of success in our lives. Because they are not urgent, they tend to be put off, delayed, or overlooked.

### Quadrant Four: Not Urgent Not Important

These are things with little to no outcome on the driving forces of our lives. They also have no deadline. These are things like entertainment, use of alcohol, hobbies, overcommitment to groups, and other things of this nature.

## THE MAKING OF AVERAGE

The way most people use their time and lack prioritization is one of the chief causes of mediocrity. Average people spend inordinate amounts of time in quadrants two and four, responding to every emergency in their life even though it had nothing to do with their goals and dreams. They can also be found regularly wasting vast amounts of time and energy on entertainment. They complete quadrant one tasks barely, if at all. They always feel under the gun and under pressure from the important things in their life.

**Success Through Priorities**

Quadrant one is essential and is happening one way or the other. Nothing needs to be done in this quadrant other than to eliminate things from it which you may have assigned there but don't actually meet the criteria.

The next step is completely eliminating the fourth quadrant. These things don't have to be done. Even when they are done, they represent no negligible outcome toward attainment of our goals. When it comes to quadrant four, we simply eliminate.

Quadrant two is the other area where we can make substantial headway in our time management. This quadrant is the quadrant of delegation. Remember, these are things which have to get done, but not necessarily by you. Hire out as much as possible off this list and take the time saved to invest into income producing activities. Hiring out tasks doesn't cost us money; not hiring them out does. It costs us the spread between the lost revenue which could have been made and the money we spent hiring out the tasks.

By eliminating quadrant four completely and reducing quadrant two substantially, we now have the time spent in quadrant two and four to invest into the important but non-urgent quadrant. They key to massive success is locked

> **YOU CAN HAVE ANYTHING YOU WANT, BUT YOU CAN'T HAVE EVERYTHING YOU WANT, AT LEAST AT THE SAME TIME.**

in your ability to shift time-spend from quadrants two and four into quadrant three. Quadrant three is where your fortune will be made and your quality of life improved, yet it is the very quadrant ignored and given the short end of the stick by almost everybody. You have one life. MAKE IT COUNT.

## Solid Yellow Lines

Now that you have created time to allocate to your quadrant three activities, one of the things which helps to stop time from shifting back into its previous quadrants is the solid yellow line. Taught to me early in my career by a great mentor and friend, the solid yellow line concept helps to create definition between priorities and protects us against unnecessary time-spends.

When you are driving down a two-lane road, the lanes are always split by a center line marking. the type of marking generally denotes whether this is a passing lane or if passing is not allowed. When you see dashed lines it's ok to pass, but when you see solid yellow lines, it means one thing—DO NOT CROSS. We need to put solid yellow lines around the important but not urgent things in our lives. Our workout and spiritual routines, time with the family, time for rest and personal development; they get scheduled in and surrounded by solid yellow lines. You don't cross them, no matter what. We have much more control of the pace and focus of our lives than we like to admit. It's time to take control of your

> **"I DON'T HAVE TIME" IS THE ADULT VERSION OF "THE DOG ATE MY HOMEWORK."**

time allocations and watch your productivity soar. It is not only possible, but necessary, to block out the most important things. When you decide to take massive action in the direction of your dream, you must master these three words: prioritize, eliminate, delegate—so you can dominate!

## Lost Time and a Found Future

"I don't have time" is the adult version of "the dog ate my homework." One of the biggest lies floating in today's culture is we don't have time. In fact, we all have the exact same amount of time. A better statement, instead of "I don't have time" would be, "I'm a poor manager of my time." One of the best exercises I share with the people I train is the 168-hour exercise. Each of us has 168 hours in a week, and we choose how to allocate them. What this exercise does is lists all the things we have to do every week. What you will do is assign the amount of time per week you spend doing things like sleeping, eating, driving, and working. After all the categories are filled in, you simply add them all together and subtract the total from 168. What remains are the lost hours, the unaccounted-for time we have every single week. What you will find is even those with the most rigorous schedules have the ability to learn virtually any new skill, start a business, or pursue a relationship in the lost time now found.

To complete the exercise, fill in the total estimated hours spent doing each of these items in a week. Then total them at the bottom.

**168 hours**

Sleep _____

Work _____

Eating _____

Showering/Hygiene _____

Driving _____

Gym _____

Family Time _____

Church _____

Errands _____

Entertainment _____

Total _____

168 – Total = _____ Found Time

## CHOICES – THE DECISION BETWEEN TWO ACTIONS

We are not born winners, we are not born losers, we are born choosers.

The million-dollar question in life: "Is this getting me closer to or further from my stated goals and dreams?" Using this one question as a litmus test for every choice we must make is almost a guarantee of success. We make choices, and our choices make us. The byproduct process, by definition, is a PASSIVE

> **WE ARE NOT BORN WINNERS, WE ARE NOT BORN LOSERS, WE ARE BORN CHOOSERS.**

PROCESS. In other words, it's naturally occurring. That's why it's so powerful. Twenty-four hours a day, seven days a week, every week, for the rest of your life, the TBAR reaction is occurring. Choices present an opportunity to ACTIVELY accelerate or decelerate this process in our life. For example, you could choose to change your thoughts and beliefs in an area to start redirecting the byproduct process. A choice TO ACT in the direction of your goal or dream will act as an accelerant. It becomes a boost to the underlying process. A choice to act in opposition to the goal or dream will slow down and, in some cases, completely negate the underlying TBAR process.

**Right and Wrong**

It's always right to do the right thing. One of the quickest ways to totally derail your TBAR process is to make a choice which violates the law or the trust of your loved ones, employees, shareholders, church members, or others who may be depending on you and your ability to live in integrity. Are you the same behind closed doors as you are in public? Are you making choices, that if discovered, would compromise your integrity, your reputation, or your ability to continue on towards your dream? Stop now, turn around, and move in the other direction. Seek counsel and get accountable to people who can move you away from destructive choices. If you wouldn't want what you are doing printed on the front page of the paper or all over social media—don't do it. So many incredible people, careers, and dreams fail due to breaches of character and integrity. It's not worth it. It takes years to build trust and only moments to destroy it, so choose wisely. My good friend and millennial multi-millionaire Mario Arrizon says it this way, "Be the example, in every situation, and at all times."

> IT TAKES YEARS TO BUILD TRUST AND ONLY MOMENTS TO DESTROY IT.

## THE BEST CHOICE

"We are kept from our goal, not by obstacles, but by cleared paths to lesser goals."

Good is the enemy of great. So many great lives are reduced to mediocrity by the abundance of good options, making the choice of the best option less and less clear. When we don't know where we are going, any path will do. So many would-be greats exhibit habitual weakness in consistently choosing what they want most instead of what they want now. Again, the question, "Will this get me closer to or further from my goals and dreams?" is a great starting point as you evaluate the options ahead of you. But what happens when the answer is "yes" to multiple choices available to you?

In his book *The One Thing*, Gary Keller discusses the idea that there is one thing and that when you do it, makes all the other things you must do either unnecessary or easier. When using this filter to run your potential choices through,

> **WE ARE KEPT FROM OUR GOAL, NOT BY OBSTACLES, BUT BY CLEARED PATHS TO LESSER GOALS.**

the hierarchy of importance or priority becomes clear. Let's say, for example, your friend calls you last minute and offers you his box seats to tonight's game. These tickets cost $400 each, and you will be courtside for potentially the biggest game of the season. You could bring along a potential prospect with you and build rapport with them, moving them toward some potential future business. You also had a training session with your mentor scheduled for this evening. Both are good things. Both will be valuable to you for different reasons. Using Gary Keller's one thing approach, will going to the game make the other responsibilities in your life easier or unnecessary? It probably won't have an impact on your family life at all. It might make one deal a little easier with the prospect you brought along but will probably have no lasting impact on the success of your business. It definitely doesn't make your business any easier.

Let's take a look at the meeting with your mentor. When you learn and develop skills from your mentor, your income probably goes up. You may be able to hire some help around the house for your spouse, making their day-to-day duties easier or unnecessary. Your skills may also help you to become more efficient and allow you more time with your family. The thinking you pick up from your mentor makes your ability to avoid and handle challenges stronger. You waste less time, and your results get better and better. It takes you less emotional effort for better results, and your business, in general, gets easier. Because of the increase in income, you were able to hire out some of your basic duties, eliminating them altogether from your to-do list. When viewed through the lens of the one thing, while you may be able to rationalize the game as being good for business and a great opportunity, it simply doesn't stand up against the meeting with the mentor. Every "competing" choice can be successfully filtered through this paradigm.

Seek counsel: I would rather eat scraps off a wise man's table than have a banquet with fools.

Whenever you face a decision that could have great weight on the outcome of your goal, your family, your finances, or your health, you should always seek the counsel of trusted mentors. They see from a different vantage point and are not clouded by the emotional attachments to the choices you must make. When it comes to career changes, relationship changes, relocation, or other large choices, the insight of tested leaders in these areas can prove invaluable. Remember, when you buy the opinions of others, you also buy their lifestyle, which is exactly why you want the opinions of your trusted mentors. By default, they are ahead of you on the path you are walking. You want what they have, so seeking their opinion on important life choices is an absolute must.

In my business, I serve as a mentor and advisor to thousands of successful entrepreneurs. Almost always before making large impact decisions, the champions I mentor will seek my counsel. They are looking for my viewpoint, wisdom, and clarity about their situation. They look for insights in the potential byproducts of their choices they may not yet see. On the other hand, many of the people who wash out of the business make these sorts of decisions all the time but never consult a mentor about the merit and direction of their choices. It's almost as if they know the choices they are making are wrong but want to be left alone to make them anyway. So many times, I've seen problems take people out of the race, which would have easily been avoided by seeking a mentor's counsel before making the choice.

If it could affect your marriage, your finances, your faith, or your fitness, it's better to play it safe rather than sorry. Your mentors are in your life for a reason. They say experience is the best teacher, but this is untrue—learning from other people's experiences is the best teacher. Experience, wisdom, and knowledge are what your mentors possess. Leverage those assets and take explosive leaps in the direction of your dream!

## URGENCY – SUCCESS LOVES SPEED

Be patiently impatient: Patient with the process and impatient with yourself to grow, read, learn, act, and become.

Most of the top performers I know exemplify this trait. Success is urgent. Massive action is urgent. They don't put it off, they do it now. One of the greatest tools you will ever develop in using the TBAR process effectively is making input action an urgent matter. Think about urgency as speed. It's about how fast you can get something started, or done, or repeated.

Consider an airplane. It only flies because the forces of lift and thrust overcome the forces of gravity and drag. Everything in the universe is subject to gravity. However, the combination of lift and thrust allow objects like airplanes to remain aloft, despite Earth's gravitational pull. For an airplane, lift is only achieved once a plane reaches a critical velocity where the force of the air passing under the wings is greater than the force of gravity keeping the plane on the ground.

This is very similar to the way in which success and achievement work. You can have the right actions (a plane), but until those actions are going fast enough (thrust), gravity and drag (life, circumstances, etc.) will hold your plane to the ground. You are probably closer than you think to some breakthrough results. You are doing the right things, your thoughts and beliefs are creating winning actions, you just aren't

> **BE PATIENTLY IMPATIENT: PATIENT WITH THE PROCESS AND IMPATIENT WITH YOURSELF TO GROW, READ, LEARN, ACT, AND BECOME.**

going fast enough yet! Increase your speed. Hit critical mass. For example, if you make one hundred sales calls, your results may be drastically different depending on whether those calls were made over a week or over a year. When done over a week, your activity and confidence rise, you pack a lot of results into a short time, and you catch the leader's attention and the attention of peers. Your results are exemplary. You start having opportunities afforded to you which were not there before. The success repeats and creates, in turn, the opportunity for even more success.

Now picture you make those same calls to the same people but do it over a year. You took a week's results and stretched them out over fifty-two weeks. You aren't breaking any records. Heck, you probably aren't meeting your quota. You feel like a loser, an under performer, and unworthy.

Here's the key—it was the EXACT SAME AMOUNT OF EFFORT, just applied FASTER. Success loves speed, and urgency is all about speed. Take the right actions and take them fast!

One of the best tools I have found to create urgency is to make games with the actions which lead to results. Early on in my career, I found out most people simply wouldn't make enough calls, enough of the time, to generate the revenue they needed to survive and would wash out of the business. My goal every day was to have all of my calls made and appointments set for the day by noon. I made it urgent. Sometimes, I would see how many appointments I could set in one hour. Then I would try to beat that hour the next hour, either with more appointments or in less time. Occasionally, I would create small wagers with other reps and compete against them for the hour. Either way, I was done, and I was done fast. I would do in a few hours what everyone else took all day to do.

What actions are you doing that you know are the right actions, but you need to be doing them faster?

Write down three actions where you can apply urgency:

1. _____

2. _____

3. _____

# CONSISTENT – AT BEING INCONSISTENT

Consistency is the bridge between goals and accomplishments. Many times, we are doing the right things. We are taking the right action but not allowing the power of consistency to compound our effort into results. Successful people do every day what average people do sometimes. There is no secret to success. It's about doing the right things all the time, not some of the time. Think about success like investing. If you take your money out of the investment, the money will stop compounding. So, it is with success. If you take a day off of the habits and actions which give you the results you want, they stop compounding.

> **CONSISTENCY IS THE BRIDGE BETWEEN GOALS AND ACCOMPLISHMENTS.**

One of the operating principles behind the TBAR truth is the autonomous nature of the outcomes. They develop naturally as the byproduct of the step before. One of the greatest tools you can leverage to accelerate the TBAR process is the formation of action habits. Habits are created by consistency, which means doing the things which need to be done so consistently that, eventually, they no longer have to be thought about. They have become habitual. As discussed earlier, most thinking today in the field of habit creation believes it requires somewhere around sixty-three days to create a habit. The problem with inconsistency is, when you miss a day at day nineteen, you don't get to start there again tomorrow. You start back at day zero. People think, "It's just one meal, it's just one meeting, it's just one day, I deserve it." And there it goes, the newly forming habit sent back to day zero. If you are tired of starting over, stop stopping. Stop the inconsistency. Ironically, our inconsistency is actually creating the habit of inconsistency. The power of your routines and daily actions is not only a byproduct of your underlying beliefs but is responsible for creating all the results in your life. I dare you to take

> **SUCCESSFUL PEOPLE DO EVERY DAY WHAT AVERAGE PEOPLE DO SOMETIMES.**

consistent action for seventy days. Why seventy? Sixty-three for the habit, and an extra week on top of that, because we never stop at the finish line. Create a habit and turn your success on autopilot.

# 18

# ACTIVITY KILLERS

**B**eliefs create actions. They also create inaction. Inaction, as opposed to incorrect action, in my experience, holds most of the responsibility for a lack of results in our lives. As discussed earlier, when we explored the concept of using TBAR to identify and isolate issues within the byproduct process, failure to take consistent or correct action is the byproduct of incorrect or inconsistent beliefs. Let's examine here a few of the beliefs which lead to inaction.

1. **Downplaying the win.** When we believe winning isn't worth playing the game, we become benchwarmers on the field of life. Sooner or later, we need to stop riding the bench in life, watching everyone else play for their dreams and start swinging for the fences. A common cause of inaction is the belief that the win really isn't as important as we built it up to be. When we downplay

> SOONER OR LATER, WE NEED TO STOP RIDING THE BENCH IN LIFE, WATCHING EVERYONE ELSE PLAY FOR THEIR DREAMS AND START SWINGING FOR THE FENCES.

the win, similar to minimizing it, we excuse ourselves from having to play. We use these beliefs to excuse and rationalize the lack of results in our life and our inactivity in trying to change. "Don't work so hard," is a fantastic reason not to give your best. "There's more to life than money," is a perfect alibi for not having any. "Who would want to look like that—he's too ripped," is a perfect reason to keep carrying around an extra thirty pounds. It seems most people who aren't winning take every opportunity to view their way of average and ordinary living as somehow pious, compared to those living a life of excellence. They become legends in their own mind, but the scoreboard of life ultimately renders the verdict—AVERAGE INSPIRES NO ONE.

2. **Blaming others or circumstances.** Believing we aren't in control of directing our future helps to excuse us from taking action to change our reality. While many times things do happen to us outside of our control, we are always in control of how we respond to them. "If this or that was just different", "If I didn't have kids", "If only I had kids", "If I didn't have so much seniority", "If I only started earlier", "If I were younger", "If I were older", "If I had more money", "If I had more experience..." Your life will NEVER be free of "if only." You must act anyway. You must control what you can control.

3. **Rewarding ourselves even when we don't win.** Why play the game when I can get the prize anyway? Today people live a lifestyle similar to that of people making two to three times what they earn by financing their lifestyle on credit. When we reward ourselves before we have earned it, our motivation to act and to achieve

> OUR RESULTS ARE ULTIMATELY OUR PERSONAL RESPONSIBILITY, NO MATTER WHAT IS GOING ON AROUND US.SO CHOOSE WISELY.

is greatly reduced. Set goals and reward yourself when the goal is achieved. If you just buy whatever you want with money you don't have because you feel like it, guess what you won't feel like—working.

4. **Worrying about what you can't control while neglecting the things you can.** Many people believe politics, conspiracies, the man, the economy, and other outside factors are the actual limits on their achievement. Instead of taking action to change our lives, we become paralyzed, thinking it doesn't really matter what we do since institution X is really just pulling the strings

of life. While there is truth that the institutions like government can have an effect on the direction of our lives, there are people who will win and people who will lose under any administration and in any type of economy. Our results are ultimately our personal responsibility, no matter what is going on around us.

## FRUSTRATIONS

*You need this moment of pain, so when you get to the top, you know what it was like to be at the bottom.*

If you're going to pursue excellence and accomplish big things, frustration is par for the course. All great leaders experience high levels of frustration. Why? Because they are warriors against the status quo. To a leader, the status quo is exactly that—frustrating. "Why don't more people see it like I do? Why don't people care like I do? Why can't people be on time like I am?" Everywhere you turn, as a leader,

> **IF YOU'RE GOING TO PURSUE EXCELLENCE AND ACCOMPLISH BIG THINGS, FRUSTRATION IS PAR FOR THE COURSE.**

looms an opportunity to get frustrated. But remember this—frustration is GOOD. Frustration is normal. So many byproduct patterns are interrupted by misinterpreted frustration. You are frustrated because you care. Frustration, when used appropriately, is one of the highest-octane fuels available to super achievers. It is what keeps them moving against the grain and attacking the status quo around them to bring change.

Winners eat disappointment for breakfast, then ask for seconds. Leaders LOVE THE TOUGHNESS. They know it's what sets them apart from everybody else. Pain, rejection, frustration, and other negative emotions are really tests. They scream to the would-be leader, "How bad do you want this?"

> **WINNERS EAT DISAPPOINTMENT FOR BREAKFAST, THEN ASK FOR SECONDS.**

More often than not, failure is a result of frustration induced self-sabotage rather than some outside force such as competition, regulation, or the direct actions of another person. As leaders, we give up the right to be negative. People want to follow EXCITED, EMOTIONALLY CONSISTENT PEOPLE. They are surrounded by emotional rollercoasters already. BE DIFFERENT.

Almost always, failure can be traced to actions taken or not taken as a byproduct of the misinterpretation of negative feedback at the belief level. For example, someone is facing a bout of rejection in their business. Instead of viewing this as an area needing focus, growth, and improvement, they misinterpret it as a reason to stop pursuing the business because they just aren't any good at it. Negative feedback, emotions, and frustrations are actually lighthouses telling us we are close to the shore of success.

> **ARE YOU FRUSTRATED? GOOD! YOU ARE EXACTLY WHERE YOU SHOULD BE.**

Are you frustrated? Good! You are exactly where you should be. Now, instead of using your negative emotion as a cop-out, use it as fuel. Let it be your guide to where you need to improve most. Negative feedback is there for a reason—to guide us and grow us into the people and leaders we need to become. Here's a key. The frustration is necessary to sustain long range growth. Success without preparation isn't success at all; it's a burden. Look at the countless numbers of people who win the lottery but within years, end up just as poor as they were before they won, except now with a host of other issues. The money would have been a blessing to someone who was prepared to handle wealth, but to the one who was unprepared, instead of a blessing, it becomes a burden. You must go through the struggle on the way to success—

> **YOU MUST GO THROUGH THE STRUGGLE ON THE WAY TO SUCCESS—IT'S WHAT MAKES YOU STRONG ENOUGH TO BEAR THE WEIGHT OF LEADERSHIP AND INFLUENCE.**

it's what makes you strong enough to bear the weight of leadership and influence. Instead of running from it, embrace it. It's not there to discourage you; it's there to reflect and redirect you towards making the necessary improvements required to really win!

**Don't wish it were easier, wish you were better.**

One of the greatest lies sidetracking would-be leaders along the byproduct process is that it should be easier. "If God really wanted me to do this, then I wouldn't be struggling so much to attain the outcome. Maybe the struggle is a sign I'm not cut out for this."
These thoughts create beliefs and byproducts which

> **IT'S NOT SUPPOSED TO BE EASIER, AND IT NEVER GETS EASIER—WE SIMPLY GET BETTER**

are destined to create the OPPOSITE outcome you are striving for. You must guard against them. "It should be easier by now, why am I still having these issues?" Here's the truth—It's not supposed to be easier, and it never gets easier—we simply get better.

Entropy is a measure of disorder. The second law of thermodynamics, which applies to any closed system (including the universe), states that everything moves towards disorder. Over time, things don't construct themselves, they deconstruct. The natural state of the world around us is to decay. Leaders, by definition, are disruptors of the disorder around them. They master organizing systems and processes. They develop people and cultures that fight back against the disorder and create order and growth. But remember this—in every way, and every day, order and growth is under attack from the relentless erosion of entropy. Organizations

> **IT'S NOT SUPPOSED TO BE EASY; IT'S SUPPOSED TO BE WORTH IT.**

don't build themselves; leaders build them. Without the effort of the leader, the culture and organization slowly start to disintegrate until they disappear completely. It's not going to be easier. Why? Because the same force of entropy that was there in the beginning is there in the middle and will be there at the end of your journey. Every moment, it is pulling you back down to where you started. It's not supposed to be easy; it's supposed to be worth it.

When we stop wishing it was easier and start wishing we were better, stronger, and more prepared to deal with the frustration and constant opposition to our dream, then we break the power of frustration in our lives. Frustration comes from unmet expectation. We need to expect challenges along the way and understand anything truly great will also demand a great price from us. There is no free lunch.

# SECTION SIX
# RESULTS

# 19

## ACHIEVING MASTERY

**E**verything around us—the quality of our life, our relationships, the condition of our health, our finances, our legacy—are results. They are all byproducts.

Success is the byproduct of excellence. Excellent thinking, excellent beliefs, and excellent action. When you think right, you believe right. When your beliefs are correct, you take the correct actions. When you take the correct actions, in enough volume, with enough PRECISION, for enough time, the results are inevitable. Byproduct thinking helps us to focus on the process which creates the result instead the result itself. It leads to reproducible, measurable, and predictable success. When we master the input, the output takes care of itself.

While we can never control the outcome directly, we can control it indirectly. We obtain this control by controlling the inputs which create the outcome. Tim Grover says, "You don't have to love the work, you just have to love the results." The issue for most along the way is they never connect the dots between the

> TRUE CHAMPIONS LEARN TO RESPECT THE PROCESS.

thoughts and the results. They don't recognize the TBAR process at work or how it systematically creates their lives. They believe the result attainable without first building the underlying input structure. True champions learn to respect the process. They may never love it, but they respect it and understand it is the source of their true greatness. Someone told me early in my career a maxim about results that I have never forgotten. "A winner starts with the end in mind and will do anything legal, ethical, and moral to get to that end. Everyone else looks for pleasant means and will accept whatever ends those means provide." A champion, someone who wins consistently, has a very clear image of the life they want to live. They search relentlessly for the inputs required to make it a reality. They don't care whether it's enjoyable, they know that the result will be.

**Mastery: Amateurs practice until they get it right. Pros practice until they can't get it wrong.**

I'm getting results, now, I need to get them consistently.

We live in an age where there is a breadth of information all around us but very little understanding. "I know, I know," is the chorus line of the average and ordinary. Give me something new, more info, new data, something else. We often confuse mental ascent with knowing. Having heard something and recollecting bits and pieces of it is not knowing. Knowing is when the information is truly ours, and we have control and use of the knowledge. Knowing is not enough; we must master if we want to be truly great. If we really believe we truly know something, there are three questions we must be able to answer affirmatively.

Question one is, "Am I doing this?"

The biggest gap in the world is the gap between knowing what to do and doing it. Everyone knows how to lose weight—we must eat less and exercise more—yet in the US, according to the Centers for Disease Control and Prevention, there are 93 million people who are drastically overweight. We all know to become more stable financially, we should save more and spend less, but there are record high levels of indebtedness and record low levels of savings. Smokers all know they shouldn't smoke, and the list goes on and on. When we "know"

> **KNOWING IS WHEN THE INFORMATION IS TRULY OURS, AND WE HAVE CONTROL AND USE OF THE KNOWLEDGE.**

something, but we don't do that thing, we don't really know it. We've heard it, but we don't know it.

When we know by doing, there is no gap between what we know and what we do. If we are not doing what we know, we must go back to the thinking level of the TBAR process and examine the thoughts we have around these things. We must also examine our beliefs. Because we are not acting on what we have heard, there is a disconnect between the thought and the action.

The second question is, "Have I mastered this?"
Mastery is where you have developed an unconscious competence at this thing. You can do it successfully without having to think about it. You should look at the activities needed to create the success byproduct you seek and ask

> **WHEN WE KNOW BY DOING, THERE IS NO GAP BETWEEN WHAT WE KNOW AND WHAT WE DO.**

yourself, "Have I mastered this task? Would others who have mastered this task agree I have mastery of it? Are there tangible results of mastery?" I have a handful of books which I read over and over. Instead of reading every pile of trash someone who has never done anything in the real-world writes, I read and re-read the works of the masters. Why? Because the book is a byproduct. They didn't succeed by writing a book; they wrote a book about what they learned on the road to success. I want to MASTER THE FEW RECURRENT IDEAS in these books, versus filling my head with surface knowledge on a wide array of information.

The third question to ask when it comes to achieving mastery is, "Do I have proof?"
Success leaves clues. The outcome of mastery is consistent, predictable success. By default, if you are not achieving the consistent success you desire, you have not mastered the input thinking, belief, and action. Period. Don't go Dunning-Kruger on us here; put in the time and effort to truly master your craft. When you do, there will be no question if you have achieved mastery. You and everyone around you will know.

# 20

# THE PROCESS FOR CONSISTENT GROWTH

## RESULTS ON PURPOSE

I originally learned the concept of plan, do, check, and adjust in a foundational book in my development called *Launching a Leadership Revolution* by Chris Brady and Orrin Woodward. In the book, they discuss a process, PDCA, whereby the user goes through an action and feedback loop, allowing for systematic course correction and refinement of the desired results.

**PDCA**

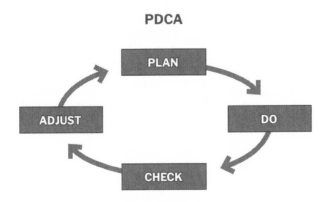

# PLAN, DO, CHECK, AND ADJUST

**PLAN:** The plan is the process of action which is assumed to create the result we want. *I will do things A, B, C, and D in this manner, for this amount of time, to create byproduct X.* When acted on, the plan will either work or will need to be adjusted.

> **MANY PEOPLE DO AND DO AND DO THEIR WHOLE LIFE AND NEVER STOP TO ASK, "IS WHAT I'M DOING WORKING?"**

**DO:** Here the action quotient discussed earlier comes into play. This is where we take action on the plan and actually do the work required by the plan.

**CHECK:** This is where we measure the outcomes created by the action. "Did I get what I wanted?" This is a critical, and commonly overlooked, part of the process. Many people do and do and do their whole life and never stop to ask, "Is what I'm doing working?" We are taught our whole lives to do something we enjoy or are good at, with little to no regard for the outcome it will produce. We must make a habit out of checking on our progress and using the data from our inspection to fuel us forward.

> **ANYTHING LESS THAN THE DESIRED GOAL MUST BE CONSIDERED A LOSS.**

If, upon inspection, we are making good progress towards our goals, then that's fantastic! Keep going. However, more times than not, honest reflection will show we aren't making as much headway as we would like. Sometimes, we are actually making no headway at all. Here, we must have courage enough to call it what it is! A loss. Anything less than the desired goal must be considered a loss.

Today, in a world where everyone gets a trophy for participating, labeling anything a loss is unheard of but is exactly what's necessary to create the win.

> **IF YOU WANT TO CREATE MASSIVE SUCCESS, YOU WILL BE CONSTANTLY PLAYING AT THE EDGE OF YOUR CAPABILITIES.**

Well-managed failure is one of the greatest causes of success, while poorly managed success is one of the greatest causes of failure. Most people are afraid of losing, but a champion knows losing is par for the course when you want to win big. If you want to create massive success, you will be constantly playing at the edge of your capabilities.

**ADJUST:** If at first you don't succeed, try doing what your coach told you to do the first time. The last part of the PDCA process is adjust, which only happens after we succeed at implementing the "check" part of the process. We can't change what we don't know needs changing. At this point in the PDCA process, it

> **IF AT FIRST YOU DON'T SUCCEED, TRY DOING WHAT YOUR COACH TOLD YOU TO DO THE FIRST TIME.**

is essential to seek feedback from the scoreboard, mentors, and resources who have more knowledge and expertise in the field. Take the input, make the adjustments, and run the process back again. PDCA is really a test of the accuracy of our thinking, believing, and actions.

Once changes have been made, the PDCA process starts all over again and pushes you towards even bigger results.

# 21

# NEXT LEVEL RESULTS

N o matter what level you are at, you can always make the decision to raise your game. When everybody else is calling it quits, the greats are usually just getting started. To elevate ourselves from one level to the next, we must start as we have started before—by challenging our current thinking with next-level thinking, next-level believing, and next-level action. The beauty of the TBAR success system is the loop can be repeated over and over again. It can be started more intentionally, and with the wisdom,

> **WHAT WE HAVE NOW IS THE BYPRODUCT OF OUR CURRENT THINKING, BELIEFS, AND ACTIONS. WHAT WE HAVE IN THE FUTURE WILL BE DETERMINED BY THE THOUGHTS, BELIEFS, AND ACTIONS OF TOMORROW.**

relationships, and resources accumulated during the last round of the process. As before, we must expose ourselves to people, thinking, and environments which call us from our current comfort zone to the next level of our purpose and destiny.

Know this, wherever you go, and whatever endeavor you may find yourself in, you now have a process to create success at whatever level you desire. What we have now is the byproduct of our current thinking, beliefs, and actions. What we have in the future will be determined by the thoughts, beliefs, and actions of tomorrow. It's time to level up. Don't just get to the top, stay at the top and redefine the game. When you get there, take an inventory of the essential areas of your life and make sure you are winning in those, too. What does it profit a man to gain the whole world and lose his soul, or his family, or his health along the way? The byproduct isn't about just winning in business, or winning in our health, it's about winning everywhere. The most incredible part of the TBAR process is, once you are obtaining the results you've dreamed of, the cycle will be running largely autonomously. Winning has become a habit in your life. Take your conscious effort now and redirect the byproduct process in other areas of your life you want to improve.

> THE BYPRODUCT ISN'T ABOUT JUST WINNING IN BUSINESS, OR WINNING IN OUR HEALTH, IT'S ABOUT WINNING EVERYWHERE.

## NOTHING FAILS LIKE SUCCESS

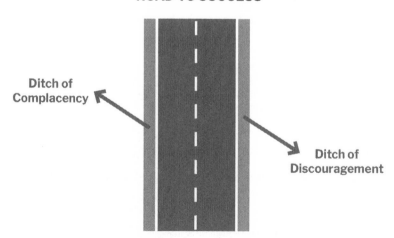

**ROAD TO SUCCESS**

Ditch of Complacency

Ditch of Discouragement

One of the dangers of success is it changes the environment we exist in. We move from the environment of hunger which created the beast and into the comforts and trappings of success that domesticates us. If we aren't careful to guard the thinking and beliefs which created our success, we are susceptible to getting soft. This is where we become so distant from who and where we were when we started; our thinking and beliefs become fundamentally different than what we had on the way up. Many people

> **MAKE NO MISTAKE—SUCCESS IN ANY AREA OF YOUR LIFE, WHETHER MARRIAGE, BUSINESS, OR ON THE FIELD, IS RENTED, AND RENT IS DUE EVERY DAY.**

starting at the bottom and hungry for success possess thoughts and beliefs which create unbelievable focus and work ethic. This, in turn, creates the success they currently enjoy. However, once they "arrive," they may begin to think the same effort and energy isn't needed to maintain their current success or reach higher levels of success. This creates beliefs they can still succeed without the same level of focus and energy. Before long, their success—their weight loss, their relationships, or their championship team—starts to struggle.

This is precisely why repeat and three-peat championships are so rare. We see this in marriages all the time, too. In the early years of the relationship, both parties worked diligently on maintaining a strong connection—bringing gifts for no real reason, planning thoughtful experiences or getaways, and looking for little ways to show the other person they are valued. Almost immediately, in some cases, after marriage, much of the effort put towards the relationship ceases. They no longer pursue, give. and sacrifice. In the beginning, there is a belief you are earning or winning this person's hand in marriage. After the marriage, the thought and belief you no longer need to earn your spouse's love and affection can creep in. Make no mistake—success in any area of your life, whether marriage, business, or on the field, is rented, and rent is due every day. The danger is the

> **NOTHING CREATES FAILURE LIKE MISMANAGED SUCCESS.**

spouse becomes familiar. The problem with this familiarity is we THINK what it took to build the relationship is no longer needed to maintain and grow the relationship. Just ask one of the 55% of people whose marriage has ended in divorce if this change in thinking, and the subsequent action and result that ensued, were accurate. We won their hand in marriage, but we lost the marriage. We won the championship but didn't make the playoffs next season. We grew the church but couldn't keep it together. This happens in virtually every area of life. It's evident in the person who lost the weight but gained it back, who built the business and then lost it, and the championship team who doesn't repeat. Nothing creates failure like mismanaged success. YOU MUST REMEMBER—success is the byproduct of the underlying thoughts and beliefs. They must be guarded and reinforced. They are, after all, creating our reality.

Take the road less traveled. It makes all the difference. It's lonely at the top. When you pay a price to be great, whether in marriage or in the boardroom or on the field, your life is going to look much different than most of the people around you. You are taking the road less traveled. Make no mistake about it, when you are relentless about improving your life, most days you will feel

> **IN A WORLD FULL OF SHORT CUTTERS, BE SOMEONE WHO GOES THE EXTRA MILE.**

like you are going down a one-way street in the wrong direction. But why fit in when you were born to stand out? Normal offers no hope, no solutions, and no dream to captivate our hearts. I don't want to be normal, and neither do you. In a world full of short cutters, be someone who goes the extra mile.

I heard a story about a home builder and his foreman. They had been working together for a long time, and it was getting close to the end of the foreman's career. As he approached retirement, he had one last build to oversee. The builder came to the foreman one day and told him, as his retirement gift, any of the money left over after building the house would be his to keep. As the construction process began, the foreman started looking for opportunities to save costs. He used thinner drywall, lower quality wiring and materials, shoddy insulation. Every step of the way, he assured himself the new owners of the house would never know the difference. At the end of the project, and almost $100,000 under budget, the builder and the foreman stood together looking at the new home. It looked beautiful on the outside, but on the inside, the foreman knew it wasn't his best work, he knew the corners he had cut. As they stood together, the foreman asked the builder, "By the way, who is this house for? I never met the owners as I was building the home." The builder turned and looked at the foreman and said, "You," as he handed him the keys. "This is your retirement gift from me to you."

The foreman had been building his own home all along. Had he known, he would have built differently. In the same way, we are building our own lives. Let's build lives we are proud of, lives that we want to live in—byproduct lives.

# 22

# IT'S WORTH IT

## THE BYPRODUCT AT WORK

A s we make up our minds, we make up our lives. A decade ago, I had nothing. I had little money and no credit. When my wife and I got engaged, I had to take her with me to the jewelry store and have her buy her own wedding ring. She put it on her credit card, and I made monthly payments to her. I would sleep until two or three p.m. every day. In the morning before she left for work, I would get up, and we would have breakfast together. After she left, I would go back to sleep and wouldn't wake up until she came home for lunch. She would come home every day because we didn't have money. After lunch, she would go back to work, and I would go back to sleep on the couch until two or three p.m. when I would finally get up and head into the music store to give guitar lessons. We were in debt, and I was seriously failing in my role to provide for my new family. Looking back now, she always tells me she took quite a gamble on me. When this happens, I gently remind her of the jackpot she hit when she did. I was thirty-five pounds overweight, an incessant worrier, and one of my best habits was consistency. Consistently, I quit everything I did. I was a starter but never finished. At twenty-three years old, I could see my future and what dreams I had slowly slipping away from me. And then, everything changed.

I learned you can't expand your own vision; someone else must do it for you. I took a job at a local church as a music director where I met someone who changed my life. He challenged my thinking, forced me to question my beliefs, and required me, as part of my employment, to read and listen to books that changed my way of thinking. He stretched my belief and saw something in me I didn't see in myself. I read, and we talked about personal responsibility and the control we really did have in directing the outcomes of our lives. For the first time, I saw myself as the driver and not just a passenger on the road of life. My thinking, my vision, and my life were all beginning to change.

Today, my life is truly incredible. We have traveled to the greatest places on earth. We have built some of the most incredible relationships with some of the most incredible people. We've made some huge differences in the lives of a lot of people. We have watched God's grace in our lives present itself in amazing ways. We have made and saved more money than I ever could have dreamed. The dream house, the dream cars, all the toys—they are all great. They are all byproducts. They are outcomes, the rewards of a decade of discipline.

The things that make life truly incredible, though, are not things at all. It's the rich and rewarding relationship I have with my wife, Jessica. It's the time I have to spend with my kids and be there as they grow up. It's happiness. It's looking in the mirror and seeing the man I was and being proud of the man I've become. My life is a byproduct. Your life is a byproduct.

At age twenty-three, I couldn't get out of bed if you paid me; today, I'm up at the same time every day and crushing the day before most people are getting theirs started. In the past, I was overweight; I hated the gym. Today, I'm my ideal weight, I workout five or six days a week and do cardio every day. A decade ago, I was dead broke; today, we are multi-millionaires. Back then I was worried and fearful of the future. Today, I know we are writing our futures. It was hard, at first, to make the changes. Today, it's just what I do. It's autonomous. It's the byproduct. I am not special. I'm not any different than you; my life is a byproduct. Yours can be too. How did I do it? The byproduct. It's how you will do it, too.

I'm not perfect, not even close. None of us are. But one thing I've always tried my best to do is to do the right things for the right reasons. I believe when you do that consistently, the world will make room for you. Be good to people, follow through on what you say you are going to do, look for those you can help along the way. It will all work out. When you do the right things when the wrong things are happening, that's what sets you apart from everybody else. Don't worry about how you are going to get "there," wherever "there" is for you. Just live this day right. Do it again tomorrow and the day after and the day after that, and one day, you will look up and years of scattering good seed has produced a harvest of health happiness and prosperity in your life. It's time to think big, upset the status quo in your life, flip the switch, let it rip, and watch the flame of greatness in your life burn uncontrollably. When your byproduct process is dialed in, your life becomes uncontainable.

What do you want out of life? Do you want to be happy? Do it. Do you want to get healthy? Do it. Do you want to double your income? Do it. Do you want to change your life? Do it. Do you want to improve your marriage? Do it. Do you want to change the world? Do it! Start now. Don't wait. Take control of the byproduct process in your life. Thoughts become beliefs—beliefs become actions—actions become results. Change your thinking, and change your life. The world is waiting.

Byproduct.

@IANPRUKNER

# ABOUT THE AUTHOR

Ian Prukner was born and raised in Royal Oak, Michigan. As a child, he was taught to attend school, get good grades, and find a good job. At 23 years old, he found himself with a college degree, a new wife, and not one job, but three, trying to make ends meet. He describes himself during this time as dying inside as the real world took a toll on him, making only $27,000 a year and working 80-90 hours a week. He knew he wasn't happy or fulfilled, and deep down, he felt that there was something more for his life and his family. He would get up every day and drive past miles and miles of magnificent homes and say to himself, "There has got to be a better way." With every day that passed, he could feel his dreams slipping away. So, he decided to make a change. Less than ten years later, with no experience in business or sales of any sort, he found himself earning in excess of seven figures annually. His life was literally revolutionized, not just financially but in every area, including health and marriage relationship. He went from watching his dreams slip away to walking in them every single day. Today, he lives in his dream home, travels the world, and raises his three incredible kids. This book BYPPRODUCT is itself, the byproduct of what he learned and applied over those 10 Years. It's what he used to drastically change everything in his life. It's a decade of leadership, learned in the trenches of American business, applied to life. This is how Ian did it.

Connect with Ian on Instagram: @ianprukner

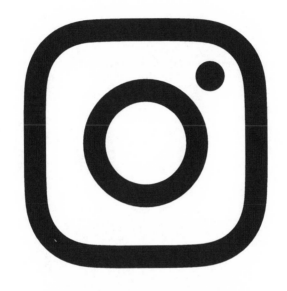

**FOLLOW @IANPRUKNER ON INSTAGRAM**

# RESOURCES

| | |
|---|---|
| DiSC assessment: | http://bit.ly/selfleadershipDISClinkorder |
| Connect with Ian: | @ianprukner on Instagram |
| Contact Us: | info@byproductbook.com |

# NOTES

Brady, Chris, and Orrin Woodward, Launching a Leadership Revolution (New York: Hachette Book Group USA, 2005.

Brault, Robert.Short Thoughts For The Long Haul. Amazon CreateSpace Independent Publishing Platform. 2017.

Centers for Disease Control and Prevention. "Adult Obesity Facts." CDC.gov. accessed April 4, 2019. https://www.cdc.gov/obesity/data/adult.html. .

Covey, Stephen R. The 7 Habits of Highly Effective People Wisdom and Insight. Philadelphia: Running Press, 1989.

DEV. "Monster." Recorded 2010. Single. 2010, CD.

"DiSC Profile - Learn about Yourself. Work More Productively." n.d. DiSCProfile. com. Wiley. Accessed May 2, 2019. https://www.discprofile.com/.

Dispenza, Joe, Breaking the Habit if Becoming Yourself. Houston: Hay House. 2013.

Forleo, Marie. 2012. How to Re-Program Your Subconscious Mind to Get What You Want w/ Dr. Cathy Collautt. Other. YouTube. How to Re-Program Your Subconscious Mind to Get What You Want w/ Dr. Cathy Collautt.

Forleo, Marie. Twitter Post. October 03, 2016, 5:39. https://twitter.com/marieforleo/status/782922910390452225.

Frankl, Viktor. Man's Search for Meaning. Boston: Beacon Press. 1959.

Garson. n.d. "Opportunity Is Missed Because It Is Dressed in Overalls and Looks Like Work." Quote Investigator. Accessed April 9, 2019. https://quoteinvestigator.com/2012/08/13/overalls-work/.

Grover,Tim, and Shari Wenk. Relentless: From Good to Great to Unstoppable. New York: Scribner, 2013.

Hill, Napoleon. Think and Grow Rich. New York: Chartwell Books, 2015.

Holy Bible: New International Version. 2018. Grand Rapids, MI: Zondervan. www.biblegateway.com.

Keller, Gary, and Jay Papasan. The ONE Thing: the Surprisingly Simple Truth behind Extraordinary Results. London: John Murray, 2014.

Kruger, Justin, and Dunning, David. . "Unskilled and Unaware of It: How Difficulties in Recognizing One's Own Incompetence Lead to Inflated Self-Assessments". Journal of Personality and Social Psychology. 77 (6): 1121–1134. 1999.

Luft, Joseph, and Harrington Ingham. "The Johari window, a graphic model of interpersonal awareness". Proceedings of the western training laboratory in group development. Los Angeles: University of California, Los Angeles. 1955.

Magness, Steve, and Brad Stulberg, Peak Performance: Elevate Your Game, Avoid Burnout, and Thrive with the New Science of Success. New York: Rodale, 2017.

Marston, William M. Emotions of Normal People. London: Kegan Paul, Trench, Trubner & Co, Ltd., 1928.

"'Our Greatest Fear Should Not Be of Failure, but of ..." n.d. Quotable Quote. Accessed April 5, 2019. https://www.goodreads.com/quotes/390887-our-greatest-fear-should-not-be-of-failure-but-of.

Robbins, Anthony. Awaken the Giant within: How to Take Immediate Control of Your Mental, Emotional, Physical & Financial Destiny! New York: Free Press, 1991.

Segal, P. 1995. Tommy Boy. Directed by L Michaels. United States: Paramount Pictures

Sharma, Robin, The Monk Who Sold His Ferrari: A Fable About Fulfilling Your Dreams and Reaching Your Destiny. New York: HarperOne. 1996.

Siebold, Steve. 177 Mental Toughness Secrets of the World Class: The Thought Processes, Habits and Philosophies of the Great Ones. London House, 2010.

St. Francis of Assisi. "The Franciscan Archive." Franciscan Sources. Accessed April 3, 2019. https://franciscan-archive.org/fontes.html

"The Retiring Carpenter – A Story About the Life We Build for Ourselves." Better Life Coaching Blog, October 21, 2011. https://betterlifecoachingblog. com/2011/09/23/the-retiring-carpenter-a-story-about-the-life-we-build-for-ourselves-2/.

"The Second World War Vol.2." Letter to Lord Wavell. 1940. Lib Quotes, November 26, 1940. https://libquotes.com/winston-churchill/quote/lbt9c0z.

41013933R00117

Made in the USA
Lexington, KY
04 June 2019